M000200645

Wessex

A Captivating Guide to an Anglo-Saxon Kingdom of England and Its Rulers Such as Alfred the Great, Edward the Elder, and Athelstan

© Copyright 2020

All Rights Reserved. No part of this book may be reproduced in any form without permission in writing from the author. Reviewers may quote brief passages in reviews.

Disclaimer: No part of this publication may be reproduced or transmitted in any form or by any means, mechanical or electronic, including photocopying or recording, or by any information storage and retrieval system, or transmitted by email without permission in writing from the publisher.

While all attempts have been made to verify the information provided in this publication, neither the author nor the publisher assumes any responsibility for errors, omissions or contrary interpretations of the subject matter herein.

This book is for entertainment purposes only. The views expressed are those of the author alone, and should not be taken as expert instruction or commands. The reader is responsible for his or her own actions.

Adherence to all applicable laws and regulations, including international, federal, state and local laws governing professional licensing, business practices, advertising and all other aspects of doing business in the US, Canada, UK or any other jurisdiction is the sole responsibility of the purchaser or reader.

Neither the author nor the publisher assumes any responsibility or liability whatsoever on the behalf of the purchaser or reader of these materials. Any perceived slight of any individual or organization is purely unintentional.

Free Bonus from Captivating History
(Available for a Limited time)

Hi History Lovers!

Now you have a chance to join our exclusive history list so you can get your first history ebook for free as well as discounts and a potential to get more history books for free! Simply visit the link below to join.

Captivatinghistory.com/ebook

Also, make sure to follow us on Facebook, Twitter and Youtube by searching for Captivating History.

Contents

Introduction

The Golden Wyvern of Wessex

https://upload.wikimedia.org/wikipedia/commons/thumb/4/47/Wessex_dragon.svg/ 1280px-Wessex_dragon.svg.png

The Anglo-Saxon Kingdom of Wessex was created through conquest by the Germanic tribe known as the Gewisse. For the following five hundred years, this kingdom went through various transformations. Some even argue that those transformations were nothing more than the natural development of a society. However, while the other Anglo-Saxon kingdoms prospered and rose to be a significant power in the region just to fall from grace and be consumed in the events of the period, Wessex pressed on. It, too, came close to its downfall when it seemed that Mercia, a neighboring kingdom, would prevail in the constant struggle for domination. However, Wessex showed that it could thrive even under the pressure of other, much stronger forces.

One of the main reasons for the success of the West Saxons was its leadership. A series of strong kings ruled this kingdom, expanding its borders, maintaining prosperous alliances, and leading their people into a better future. Wessex was one of the richest kingdoms, and it is no wonder that law and education prospered here. The kings of Wessex understood the significance of the written word, and it is from here where most of the written records come, and these records survived the ages to tell us their stories.

The *Anglo-Saxon Chronicle*, written at the court of King Alfred the Great, is one of the main sources of information for scholars about the entirety of medieval England. Alfred's law code gives insight into the laws of the previous kings of Wessex but also those of Mercia and Kent. The medieval West Saxon rulers understood the significance of the world around them. They gathered and preserved information about significant people and other kingdoms that interacted with their own. Due to the marvelous work of the West Saxon monks and scribes, we can put the pieces together and create a large picture of what medieval England was like.

Wessex started its expansion during the 8th and 9th centuries, and at first, it encompassed all the lands south of the Thames. The kings of the West Saxons became overlords to all the smaller kingdoms around their heartland. Some were absorbed into Wessex while others continued being independent, although they had to recognize the authority of the kings of the West Saxons. Some were still defiant, but it wasn't long until the Vikings arrived as well. The Danish raids altered any plans the kings of Wessex might have had about continuing their expansion. The pillaging and notorious brutality of the Vikings left a deep scar in the Anglo-Saxon world. Some kingdoms were unable to defend themselves, while others bought their peace. One by one, the Anglo-Saxon kingdoms fell once the Danes changed the nature of their attacks from raids to organized warfare. They were here to stay and work the land, as well as raise their families. England had only two options—to succumb or to defy the newcomers.

The first to fall was East Anglia, followed by Northumbria and Mercia. Wessex remained as the last Anglo-Saxon kingdom, and if it wasn't for the capable leadership of Alfred the Great, it too would have fallen. And what a sequence of events that was. Alfred was the youngest of five brothers, so he shouldn't have had any chance to rule. However, a series of events that occurred made it possible for this young scholar-king to take the throne. With the keen mind he had, Alfred realized he wouldn't be able to defend his kingdom if a change in the Anglo-Saxon world didn't happen. His reorganization of the army and the whole kingdom led to a decisive victory over the Vikings. He didn't just beat the Danes: Alfred the Great set the scene for further conquest. He created the opportunity for his successor to go even further in their intentions and unite the kingdom, which was an opportunity Athelstan recognized and took seriously. England was united, and even though it would face the challenges of renewed Viking attacks, the Anglo-Saxon kingdoms would always strive to unite in the future.

And what of Wessex? It survived. Wessex transformed from a Germanic pagan kingdom to the center of power in the whole of England. It is a kingdom that continues to inspire even today. Wessex still exists as a historical and geographical region, sparking respect through its symbols and representation. A golden dragon is still flying, commemorating the former glory of a past kingdom.

Timeline

410: Western Roman Emperor Honorius officially declares that the cities of Britain need to take care of their own defenses. The end of direct Roman rule in Britain.

Late 4th century: The Anglo-Saxons launch their raids in Britain.

Circa 490: The Battle of Badon; Celtic British win against the Anglo-Saxons.

495: Cerdic comes to Britain.

519: Cerdic founds Wessex and reigns as its first king.

534: Cerdic dies and is succeeded by Cynric.

Circa 560: Cynric dies; Ceawlin becomes the king of Wessex.

592: The Battle of Woden and the building of the Wansdyke. Separation of Anglo-Saxons in the east and the rest of Britain.

592: Ceawlin is deposed; Ceol becomes king of Wessex.

597: Ceol dies; Ceolwulf inherits the throne of Wessex.

611: Cyneglis becomes king of Wessex.

628: The Battle of Cirencester, where Cyneglis was defeated by Penda of Mercia.

630: Cyneglis is baptized; Wessex becomes a Christian kingdom.

642: Cenwealh takes the throne of Wessex and marries Penda's sister, Seaxburh.

672: Cenwealh dies; his widow becomes the first and only woman to rule Wessex.

674: Escwine becomes the king of Wessex.

676: Centwine takes the throne of Wessex.

685: Caedwalla becomes king of Wessex. He attacks Sussex and the Isle of Wight and commits genocide on the island.

686: Caedwalla takes control over Kent.

689: Caedwalla abdicates and leaves for Rome, where he dies. Ine becomes king of Wessex.

694: Ine writes the Wessex law.

705: Wessex gains control over Surrey.

710: Ine fights against Dumnonia.

715: The Battle of Woden's Barrow.

722: Ine attacks Sussex. Wessex loses the Battle of Hehil against the Britons.

726: Ine abdicates the throne and leaves for Rome. Ethelheard becomes king of Wessex.

733: Mercia invades Wessex and takes Somerset. Mercia's overlordship of Wessex begins.

740: Cuthred becomes king of Wessex.

750s: Wessex gains independence.

756: Cuthred dies.

757: Cynewulf becomes king of Wessex. Ethelbald of Mercia dies; Cynewulf retrieves the northern Wessex territories.

779: The Battle of Bensington, where Wessex is defeated by Offa of Mercia.

786: Beorhtric becomes king of Wessex under the overlordship of Offa.

802: Beorhtric dies; Ecgberht is crowned king of Wessex.

815: Wessex attacks Dumnonia.

825: The Battle of Ellandun; Wessex defeats Mercia.

829: Ecgberht invades Mercia and drives its king into exile.

830: Mercia regains independence.

836: The Vikings attack Wessex. The Battle of Carhampton takes place, which Ecgberht loses against the Danes.

838: The Battle of Hingston Down takes place, which Wessex wins against the Vikings. Wessex annexes Dumnonia.

839: Ecgberht dies; Ethelwulf becomes king of Wessex.

849: Alfred the Great is born.

850 or 855: Ethelwulf goes on a pilgrimage to Rome and brings Alfred with him. Wessex co-ruled by Ethelwulf and his son, Ethelbald.

851: The Vikings attack Wessex; Ethelwulf defeats them.

858: Ethelwulf dies; Wessex is divided with Ethelbald ruling Wessex and Ethelberht ruling Kent.

860: Ethelbald dies; Ethelberht takes the throne. Ethelberht unites Wessex and Kent once more.

865: Ethelred I, Ethelbald's and Etherlberht's younger brother, becomes king of Wessex.

866: The Vikings conquer York and Northumbria.

867: Mercia comes under Viking attack.

869: The Vikings attack and conquer East Anglia.

870: The Vikings attempt to invade Wessex but are expelled from the kingdom.

871: Ethelred I dies; Alfred, Ethelred's younger brother, becomes the king of Wessex.

874: The Vikings expel King Burgred from Mercia.

876: Renewed Viking attacks. Alfred is unable to repel them.

878: The Vikings attack Wessex; Alfred escapes. Later in the year, Alfred wins in the Battle of Edington against the Vikings.

878: Alfred the Great and Guthrum make a treaty. Guthrum accepts Christianity and takes the name Ethelstan. The treaty also defines the borders of the Danelaw, and Alfred becomes the king of the Anglo-Saxons.

888: Guthrum dies.

892: The Vikings attack Wessex.

896: Alfred builds a fleet and defeats the Vikings, who give up on conquering Wessex.

899: Alfred dies; Edward the Elder becomes the king of Wessex.

902: Battle of Holme after Ethelwold, Edward's cousin, and the Vikings invade Mercia. The Vikings win.

906: Edward makes peace with the Danes.

909: Wessex and Mercia attack the border of Northumbria.

910: The Battle of Tettenhall takes place; the Northumbrian Vikings submit to Edward.

918: Ethelfled, Lady of the Mercians, dies; the Mercians submit to Edward.

924: Edward dies; Athelstan, Edward's son, becomes the king of the Anglo-Saxons.

926: Athelstan meets with Sitric Cáech, the king of the Vikings in Northumbria. Athelstan receives submission of the Northumbrian Vikings.

927: Athelstan becomes king of the English; Wessex is no more.

929: Athelstan dies; the united English Kingdom falls apart.

Chapter 1 – The Transitional Period

Even though the Roman rule of Britain ended in the early 5th century, their presence remained in the form of education, law, and economy, and it was the elite of the British society that insisted on old Roman traditions. They rebuilt Roman villas and baths, and they, at times, even built completely new ones that were still based on Roman designs. Water ran through the pipes of households during the sub-Roman period. Literacy in the Latin language survived mainly because of the dominant religion of Christianity. However, it was the elite's insistence of continuing the Roman way of life that helped maintain Latin influence beyond the Church.

Even though the Western Roman Empire, to which Britain belonged, withdrew all their troops from the island, the majority of its inhabitants considered themselves to be Romans. As such, Britain continued to be a part of the culture that was the Roman world. It's possible the Anglo-Saxons were already present in Britain during this sub-Roman period as mercenaries who were called to help fight off the "barbarian attacks" of 408. This transitional period of Britain between the Roman rule and the rule of the Anglo-Saxons is usually observed as a period of Britain's decline. But not all of Britain suffered the same fate at the same time. Different parts had different problems to deal with, as well as different methods of survival in order to cope.

For some time, Wessex continued its Romanized everyday life. The evidence suggests that Winchester continued to be one of the major towns or forts of this region. During the 4th century, this town was flourishing as it attracted not only the merchants and craftsmen but also by the elites of the society, who built their rich residencies on the outskirts. However, with the decline of Roman rule in Britain, these residencies, together with the villas in the countryside, were either abandoned or repurposed into storage rooms. Wessex may have experienced a major economic crash during the early 5th century, and it was easier for its people to go back to a simpler way of life.

The towns of Wessex didn't just simply cease to exist, however. They continued to prosper well into the 5th century, but signs of the decline of town life can be seen shortly after. Archeologists discovered a layer of black earth covering the villas on the outskirts of Winchester and similar towns in Wessex. This is a sure sign of the decomposition of Roman timber used to build these villas, as well as the plant life overgrowing on top of it. The same was the fate of Roman pottery and tools. However, people didn't just stop using them. They continued to use them in the British Isles well beyond the early 5th century. However, these items were not produced anymore. It was not because people didn't know how but because they needed to revert to more simplified versions to be able to afford their production. Britain didn't enter a downfall due to the fact the Romans left; rather, it was due to the economic crisis that followed, and many historians speculate that it would have happened even if Rome continued to rule.

The late 4th century had seen the increase of taxes in the British Isles, which were imposed by Roman emperors who fought wars in faraway lands. Small farmers had to overproduce to be able to pay these taxes, and the majority simply couldn't keep up with the demand. In the cities and among the elite, the economic crash wasn't felt at first, probably because it was in these cities where the coin circulation had to continue. Also, it is the elite of the society who collected the taxes, which most likely helped them to accumulate their wealth too. However, the more the Roman demand for taxes grew, the more the British economy suffered, causing the collapse of its society. Even the cities were not able to keep up with the demand, and they, too, started their downfall. Once the Roman influence vanished, so did the trade they brought with them. Many previously wealthy families of merchants and town administrators had to settle for much simpler lives. Plenty of them even abandoned the cities in search of food in the countryside.

In Wessex, specifically, all regions suffered equally, and as such, the disappearance of the Roman way of life affected them all. It is, therefore, not safe to presume that the arrival of the Germanic tribes to the shores of eastern Wessex was the event that sparked the change. In fact, the change had started much earlier with the economic crisis and the abandonment of the Roman way of life.

But Germanic tribes did bring another change with them. They might not have directly influenced the downfall of Romanized Britain, but they did affect its material culture and social values. This new influence is evident when we compare early 5th-century burial sites of eastern Wessex to western Wessex. The shires of the western territories, such as Devin, Dorset, and Somerset, lack the burial sites of the Germanic type, while eastern territories, such as Berkshire, Hampshire, and the Isle of Wight, have them dating from the late 4th century. This is why the eastern and western territories of Wessex have to be regarded separately when it comes to the pre-Saxon period.

The Arrival of the Anglo-Saxons

https://en.wikipedia.org/wiki/Angles#/media/File:Britain_peoples_circa_600.svg

Gildas the Wise, a monk who lived and worked in 6th century Britain, wrote *De Excidio et Conquestu Britanniae* ("On the Ruin and Conquest of Britain"), a religious tract in which he blames the downfall of Britain after the Romans left on the non-Christian lives of his contemporaries. Even though his work is not regarded as history but as a religious sermon, he does mention the Saxons as an overseas enemy who brought harsh judgment on his people, a judgment they deserved for not following the Christian doctrine. Gildas gives us an explanation of how the Saxons came to be in Britain in the first place as well. After the Romans left, Britain suffered from the attacks of the Scots and Picts, and in order to defend their territories, a council of local rulers, which Gildas calls "the tyrants," decided to give the eastern lands to the Saxons in exchange for their protection. The late

4th-century burial sites of eastern Wessex suggest that it could be this territory that was given to the Saxons initially. The main ruler of the council was a man who Gildas named "superbus tyrannus" (which may be translated as the arrogant or proud tyrant), and he is identified as King Vortigern in later sources.

Gildas also informs us that the Saxon mercenaries who inhabited the eastern territories complained about the lack of food. When the kings of Britain didn't listen and refused to send them food, they broke the treaty and attacked the territories across the whole of Britain. The first war between the Saxons and Britain lasted for nearly thirty years, starting with the Battle of Badon. Gildas tells us he was born in the year of this battle, which makes him the source who might have had firsthand information on the events. The battle was a victory for the Britons (Britons were the Celtic people native to the British Islands), and they successfully stopped the spread of Anglo-Saxons throughout Britain. Legend has it that the mythical King Arthur participated in this battle. Sadly, the lack of sources makes it almost impossible to conclude the exact date, location, and other details regarding this battle.

By Gildas's account, it was Ambrosius Aurelianus who led the Britons to victory in the Battle of Badon. He was a military leader and a Christian whose parents were slaughtered in the initial Saxon attack. He gathered other survivors of Saxon raids and formed an army mighty enough to stop their further conquest of Britain. Ambrosius is the only man from the 5th century who Gildas mentions by name. It is important to mention that it wasn't Gildas who linked King Arthur to the Battle of Badon, though. The Arthurian legend comes from the 9th century, and its author is possibly a Welsh monk named Nennius, who certainly didn't live at the time of this battle; therefore, he is not a reliable source.

What followed the Battle of Badon was an extensive period of peace, in which Gildas lived. It was this peace that brought the unjust rule of tyrants who lived in luxury and self-indulgence. The criticism

Gildas made in his work *De Excidio et Conquestu Britanniae* was pointed toward his contemporaries, and it is no wonder he does not name all of them. He does name some, though, and in doing so, he attached an insult to the name. For example, he speaks of a certain Aurelius Caninus (Aurelius the Dog-like), but we cannot connect this name to any of the known kings who ruled Britain during this period. This is because, for Gildas, the historical facts were just a byproduct of his sermon. Instead, he intended to speak up against the rule of kings. And he did not limit himself to one kingdom; he was concerned with the whole of Britain, regardless of language or ethnicity.

Gildas also complained about the partition of the country, as its eastern parts were given to the enemy. Shrines in the Saxon territories were unavailable to the pilgrims of Breton origin (Celtic people native to the historical region of Brittany, today's western France), and this is where Gildas sees the fall of his country. He blames the leaders for abandoning the eastern parts, but he also calls for a civil war or an uprising of the people to bring justice back to the territories that were still under their claim.

The second source widely used by historians to interpret the events regarding the settling of the Anglo-Saxons is Bede's *Historia ecclesiastica gentis Anglorum* (the "Ecclesiastical History of the English People"), which dates to around 731 CE. Bede carries the title of the "Father of English History" because his works, even though filled with biblical commentary, are historical in nature. He used Gildas's writing as his source but also other contemporary writers that did not survive. Bede was a Northumbrian, and so, his work is biased as he wrote with the intent to represent other Anglo-Saxon kingdoms in a worse light. However, his division of the Anglo-Saxon settlement in three phases might have a better historical background than Gildas's suggestion of an invasion.

Bede speaks of the exploration phase, in which the Saxons came to Britain as mercenaries on the invitation of the warlord Vortigern, who employed them to defend the kingdom from Scots and Picts. After the exploration phase came the migration phase. Twenty-first-century scholars have developed a theory that states a great migration of the peoples happened due to climate change. It was this climate change that was responsible for the lack of food in the Anglo-Saxon country of origin, as well as possible floodings, which urged the people to migrate and seek new lands. The third phase, Bede explains, started when the newcomers, the Anglo-Saxons, took control over the territories of Britain. This is the phase in which the Saxons gained political dominance over the Bretons.

The only source of Anglo-Saxon origin that speaks of their migration and settlement on the British Isles is the *Anglo-Saxon Chronicle*, which dates from the 9th century. More precisely, the original manuscript was created during the reign of King Alfred the Great, probably in Wessex. However, none of the manuscripts that survived are originals. The *Anglo-Saxon Chronicle* is a collection of manuscripts, and they are all copies of one original, which were then distributed to various monasteries for preservation and further updates. Some continued to be updated even six hundred years after the original was created. Even though it is a historical document, it is hard to discern which version is to be trusted as the manuscripts differ from each other, even when they are mentioning the same events. But the advantage of the *Anglo-Saxon Chronicle* is that it notes some events that were unknown to Gildas or Bede. These events are used to fill in the gaps and offer alternative views when studying Anglo-Saxon history.

No matter which of the sources is taken into consideration, all of them agree that the eastern territories were given to the Saxons and that it was where they based their invasion of the rest of the country. There is evidence that would support this division of Bretons in the west and Saxons in the east. Around the same year as the Battle of Woden (592), a dike was built that separated the eastern Saxon lands from the rest of Britain. This dike is known as Wansdyke, which comes from the Saxon Woden's Dyke, and it is an earthwork that served as the border between the British Celts and the West Saxons. Modern archeology suggests that the dike was built at a much earlier time, and its sections date from the Roman period. That would mean that when the Saxons took control of the land, they just renamed the existing dikes in honor of their God Woden, also known as Odin.

The Earliest Anglo-Saxon Territories and Culture

Three Germanic tribes settled in Britain: the Angles, Jutes, and Saxons. The *Anglo-Saxon Chronicle* speaks about a legend that says they came in three ships, each landing in a different place in Britain. The Angles landed on the territories that would later be known as East Anglia, Northumbria, and some parts of Mercia. The Jutes came to the lands known as Kent and the Isle of Wight, while the Saxons took over what would become Wessex and southern Mercia. However, the Britons made no distinction between these Germanic tribes, and Gildas named them all Saxons. Later, Bede used the term "Angli" to describe all three tribes. The Anglo-Saxon name came into use during the 8th century when the need to distinguish continental Saxons from those of England arose. Anglo-Saxon came to mean English Saxons, and as such, it has been in use ever since. The Christian Church preferred the term "Angli" for the people, and it stayed in use even during the reign of King Alfred the Great (r. 871–899) of the West Saxons.

Anglo-Saxons rarely called themselves by this name, though. They made tribal differences, and at the beginning of their settlement of Britain, they used local clan names such as Mierce, Cantie, Gewisse, Westseaxe, and so on. Some of these names would be preserved in the geographical names of kingdoms or towns. In fact, it was the Angli who gave the name to modern-day England, and their language, Englisc, known to us as Old English, went through modernization to become today's English language.

Within Wessex, it was the valley of the River Thames that offers the earliest evidence for Germanic settlement. Some historians speculate it was the clan or the tribe named Gewisse that originally inhabited these parts of Britain and that the term West Saxons came into use at a later date when this tribe took control of other peoples who inhabited the area. The River Thames and its surroundings became what would later be the traditional heart of power for the Anglo-Saxon kingdoms. It is almost impossible to tell the exact borders of each of the tribe's domains, though, as they often fluctuated over time. In the same manner, it is impossible to pinpoint a date when any of the Anglo-Saxon kingdoms started its existence.

The first ruler of the Gewisse tribe that Bede mentions in his *Historia ecclesiastica gentis Anglorum* is Ceawlin, but he also observed that he was the second of the great overlords. This means he had a predecessor who was probably as equally powerful as he was. However, all Anglo-Saxon royal families tended to spread the belief that they had an ancestor who was a famous hero and who was probably somehow related to Woden. The Mercian royal house has a mythical ancestor Icel who was supposedly the one who led the great migration. The East Anglian dynasty claims they are the descendants of Wehha, who was possibly a hero from the old English poem *Beowulf* and who was tied to the old Swedish royal family. The house of Wessex originates from the hero Cerdic, the first king of Wessex. The *Anglo-Saxon Chronicle* claims he was a direct descendant of the god Woden.

The Anglo-Saxon tribes started uniting into kingdoms sometime during the 5th century. It is widely believed that it was the position of the Anglo-Saxon peasants that created the opportunity for the beginning of kingship. The Anglo-Saxon peasant, known as a ceorl, was a free man with certain rights, such as protection under the law and owning land. A ceorl had his kinsmen as support, and he worked the land but also carried arms in times of need. The ceorls were grouped around one overlord to whom they paid rent or provisions in return for leadership during crises. It was these groupings of working individuals that created the basis for the existence of kingdoms.

Larger kingdoms were established by the end of the 6th century, first on the southern and eastern shores of Britain. Although the exact borders are not known, they included the Jutes of Hampshire and Wight, the South Saxons, the East Saxons, and the Angles of Lindsay, Deira, and Bernicia (lands north of the River Humber, which would later become Northumbria). It is possible that these kingdoms created their first bases on territories that were previously occupied by the Romans. It may be that they used the old Roman network of roads and towns. By the end of the 6th century, the Anglo-Saxon overlords started acting as kings. Bede uses the term *bretwalda* to describe a warrior leader who had dominion over a group of people and who was able to establish a system of tribute payments. The *bretwalda* also offered protection to the small regions that were inhabited by people who paid him tribute. All Anglo-Saxon *bretwaldas* claimed their descendancy from Woden one way or another, making it seem as if it was a condition of some sort when imposing their rule over others.

Anglo-Saxons were pagans when they came to Britain, as they had brought their religion with them. By the time of the Anglo-Saxon arrival, Britain was already accepting Christianity. During the late 4th century, Christianity had its centers in the major towns. But in the countryside, the old Celtic polytheistic religion still bloomed. Some areas of Wales lacked any evidence of Christianity until the early 5th century. With the arrival of the Anglo-Saxons, the Britons who mingled with them adopted their religion as a way of progressing in society. Anglo-Saxon paganism is probably the same as the belief system of other northern European countries. Sadly, there is no written contemporary evidence as the first Anglo-Saxon settlers were illiterate. The only source for their pagan religion we can find is in the writings of later Christian monks. However, they never described the pagan belief system of the Anglo-Saxons as they were not interested in it. Their goal was to represent it as evil, and as such, they didn't bother to go in-depth while describing it. Other sources that can help to determine the old pagan religion of the Anglo-Saxons are mostly of archeological nature. The most evidence we have today comes from the excavation of Anglo-Saxon burial sites.

The conclusion is that the Anglo-Saxon tribes believed in deities known as *ese*, with Woden (Odin) being the most prominent. Other significant gods were Thunor (Thor) and Tiw (Tyr). All the names of the gods are the Germanic version of the old Norse religious system. The Anglo-Saxons also believed in many other supernatural beings, such as elves and dragons, which helped them explain natural phenomena. The Anglo-Saxon belief system probably included the practice of some form of shamanism, which was probably deeply rooted in magic and witchcraft. The Anglo-Saxon kingdoms converted to Christianity during the 7th and 8th centuries, though, with each kingdom doing so at its own pace.

Chapter 2 – The Creation of the Kingdom of Wessex

According to the *Anglo-Saxon Chronicle*, the first king of Wessex was Cerdic, who was one of the first settlers to come to Britain. Cerdic and his son Cynric landed with their five ships on the shores of Britain in 495, where today's Hampshire lies. Upon arriving, they fought the Briton king Natanleod at Natanleaga. Cerdic and his Saxons were victorious, although the fighting lasted for thirteen years. In 508, they killed Natanleod along with his five thousand soldiers. Cerdic founded Cerdicesleag, which is presumed to be today's Charford, where, in 519, the Anglo-Saxons defeated the Britons. Tradition has it that Charford means "Cerdic's ford" and that Natanleaga is today's village of Netley Marsh in Hampshire. However, scholars believe that King Natanleod never existed as his name is a product of etymological reinterpretation. Indeed, Natanleaga was the name of a geographical territory, and its element *naet* means wet, as this area was a marsh. This doesn't mean there was no Briton king to defeat. It simply means that his name was not preserved.

Historians don't rely heavily on the *Anglo-Saxon Chronicle* when it comes to the founding of the Wessex royal dynasty for the simple reason that archeological evidence supports the Jutes to be the first settlers of these regions. The *Chronicle* is not consistent, and some of its manuscripts describe the same events differently. For example, in some versions, the Jutes were given the Isle of Wight by Cerdic's son, Cynric, who was their ally. In another version, the Jutes' first kings, Wihtgar and Stuf, were Cerdic's nephews, while the third version claims the Jutes first landed on the Isle of Wight with King Wihtwara as their leader. Wessex was also supposedly founded by the Germanic tribe Gewisse, but this name simply means "ally." One theory suggests that the Gewisse were, in fact, the allies of the Jutes, but whether it was another Germanic tribe or the Britons remains unclear.

The name of King Cerdic is also problematic as it seems to be of Brittonic origin. Scholars think of it as a Germanic form of the Briton name Ceretic, which is a familiar Celtic name (for instance, Ceretic of Alt Clut was the king of Scotland from the 5th century). One theory is that Cerdic was a native Briton whose family integrated into the Anglo-Saxon society very early, possibly even as early as the 4th century. This theory is supported by the fact that some of Cerdic's descendants also had Briton names, such as Cedda or Caedwalla (Cædwalla). The other possibility is that Cerdic comes from the Anglo-Saxon family who inhabited Britain before the great migration and who accepted this Celtic influence. This would explain his familiarity with the Anglo-Saxon society well enough to become their leader but still be influenced enough by the Britons to keep their name and to even pass it on to his descendants.

When the *Anglo-Saxon Chronicle* first mentions Cerdic and his son Cynric, it names them as ealdormen, and it binds them to the year of 495. It is possible that they were the representatives of an old Briton noble family that possessed the lands that were under Anglo-Saxon attacks. As ealdormen, they were tasked to defend these lands, and this element of the *Chronicle* supports the theory that Cerdic and the dynasty he founded in Wessex was, in fact, of Briton origin. As an independent ruler, Cerdic is mentioned only in 519, which suggests that this was when he ceased being a Briton vassal and started his own kingdom. It is possible that Breton Cerdic developed blood relations with the invading Saxons and Jutes, who named him and his men

"Gewisse", or "allies." Some scholars even go further to prove Cerdic's Briton origin and claim his father was Elesa or Elasius, who was the chief of the region during Roman Britain. There is a minority among historians who believe that Cerdic is a purely fictional character who was created by later Anglo-Saxon kings of Wessex to justify their family ties with Woden and the territories they ruled.

Once Cerdic began his rule, he tried to expand his kingdom. There is evidence that suggests the Saxons attacked a British stronghold, Badbury Rings, across the River Avon. It seems that the attack was unsuccessful, and the expansion of Cerdic's Wessex was halted for the next thirty to fifty years. It is possible that at the same time the Battle of Badon happened, the peace agreement between the Anglo-Saxons and the Britons was achieved. This would certainly stop any further attempt of the expansion, at least for the time being. Even though Gildas claims the Saxons were defeated in this major battle, the *Chronicle* fails to give any report about the defeat.

The *Anglo-Saxon Chronicle* notes that Cerdic died in 534 and that he was succeeded by his son, Cynric, but the Genealogical Regnal List, which is a preface to the *Chronicle*, mentions a certain Creoda. It is possible that Cynric was, in fact, Cerdic's grandson and that his actual son, Creoda, ruled very shortly. Because his name is never mentioned in the body of the *Chronicle*, some scholars claim he never existed and that his name is just an addition to the list of rulers to expand the royal family.

The origins of the Kingdom of Wessex are more complex than what surviving sources of later dates suggest. We cannot truly pinpoint the date of the beginning of Cerdic's rule simply because the *Chronicle* is a very unreliable document with many versions that contradict each other. Some historians even suggest that Cerdic ruled from 538 until 554 based on what the written sources claim. Others suggest that Cerdic was a Saxon leader who was defeated at the Battle of Badon, which could have happened anywhere between 490 and 518. Certainly, Wessex was an independent kingdom with well-defined borders by the time of the rule of King Ceawlin, who was the son of Cynric. Bede even names Ceawlin as a *bretwalda.*

The expansion of the Kingdom of Wessex continued during the rule of Cynric, who conquered Wiltshire and captured Old Sarum near Salisbury in 552. Together with his son, Ceawlin, he defeated the Britons at Beranburh, also known as Beran Byrg (possibly Barbury Castle), in 556. All of this was noted in the *Anglo-Saxon Chronicle,* the same document that claims Cynric arrived in Britain with his father Cerdic in 495. If all of these years are correct, then King Cynric cannot possibly have been the son of Cerdic, making the rule of King Creoda seem more plausible. However, scholars believe that the dates are not to be trusted as they differ greatly from manuscript to manuscript.

The name Cynric is obviously of Anglo-Saxon origin as it can be directly translated to "kin-ruler." But his predecessor Cerdic and his successor Ceawlin both had Celtic names. In order to fit the narrative, some scholars proposed an alternative etymology of Cynric's name. They claim it is a derivative of the Breton name *Cunorix,* which means "Hound-king." This name already has a history of transforming into the Old Welsh *Cinir* and in the Middle Welsh *Kynryr.* However, there is a theory that claims that Ceawlin was not Cynric's son and that the connection was made to tie the ruling Breton family with the Anglo-Saxon name. It is possible they were relatives through the blood-ties of Britons and Anglo-Saxons who intermingled during this period. This blood tie was later transformed into a father-son relationship in order to legitimize the Wessex dynasty.

Ceawlin and the Expansion of the Kingdom of Wessex

Cynric ruled for 26 years, and Ceawlin inherited the throne at around 581, although the exact year is unknown. Ceawlin ruled at the end of the 6th century, and his role in the final conquest of Britain is of key importance. It is in the *Anglo-Saxon Chronicle* that we can find the details of some of the important battles that gave Wessex its first form. Ceawlin was the leader of these campaigns, which occurred along the River Thames Valley going as far as Surrey in the east and to the west at the mouth of the River Severn. The dates of the battles are noted in the *Chronicle*, but it seems they are inaccurate, which is often the case when it comes to this document.

In 554 (according to the *Chronicle*), Ceawlin fought his first battle against the Britons at Beran Byrg (Bera's stronghold) with his father, Cynric. However, Ceawlin was the king during the next battle, which occurred in 568 at Wibbandun (current location unknown). In this battle, he fought King Ethelberht (Æthelberht) of Kent, which made this battle the first conflict between the Saxons. All previous battles recorded by the *Anglo-Saxon Chronicle*, Bede, or even Gildas are battles between Anglo-Saxons and Britons. At Wibbandun, Ceawlin was victorious, and he drove his enemy back to Kent.

In 571, a certain Cuthwulf fought a battle against the Britons at Bedcanford. During the battle, he conquered Limbury, Aylesbury, Benson, and Eynsham, but he also lost his life. It is unknown what relation Cuthwulf was to Ceawlin, but it is presumed they were of the same royal line of West Saxons. The territories that were acquired during this campaign are all mentioned to be Breton, but it is very strange that the Bretons held any lands so far to the east during this period. It has been suggested that Cuthwulf simply reconquered the territories that were lost during the Battle of Badon.

According to the *Anglo-Saxon Chronicle*, in 577, Ceawlin, together with a man named Cuthwine, killed three Breton kings—Coinmail, Condidan, and Farinmail—in Dyrham. With the death of these three kings, the West Saxons took the cities of Gloucester, Cirencester, and Bath. It is unknown who these three Breton kings were, as their names are in the archaic form and possibly transcribed from an earlier source that is lost to us. This battle must have been the key moment in the West Saxon expansion as the Britons were now divided west of Severn from their people who lived south of the Bristol Channel. This is the same territory Wessex later lost to Penda of Mercia, probably in 628, who then founded the Kingdom of Hwicce.

The last recorded victory of the West Saxons under the leadership of Ceawlin was in 584. This was the Battle of Fethan Leag, after which Ceawlin took many towns. It is speculated that Fethan Leag is, in fact, a forest named Fethelee, which used to be in the territory of today's Oxfordshire.

In his *Historia ecclesiastica*, Bede mentions Ceawlin as the second to hold imperium over the kingdoms south of the River Humber. The term "imperium" is freely translated as "overlordship," and this would mean that Bede considered Ceawlin a *bretwalda*. This is confirmed later in the *Anglo-Saxon Chronicle*, which contains a list of all of Bede's *bretwaldas* with the addition of the later king of Wessex, Ecgberht. Bede also tells us that Ceawlin was a pagan and that he was not Christianized. The first to do so was Ethelberht of Kent, who lived at approximately the same time as Ceawlin. Ethelberht is listed as the next *bretwalda* in Bede's work, but this doesn't mean he ruled after Ceawlin. Their rules probably overlapped at some point, as we have evidence that they warred against each other in 568, at least according to the *Anglo-Saxon Chronicle*. It was after this battle that Ethelberht managed to gain enough power to be considered a *bretwalda*. It might be that Ceawlin's defeat in 592 brought the opportunity for the king of Kent to rise to power.

The year 593 is noted as the year of Ceawlin's death. The *Chronicle* speaks of a great battle at Woden's Barrow (today's Adam's Grave in Wiltshire), where Ceawlin was defeated in 592, with his death following the next year. There is no mention of who his enemies were, nor are any other details of the battle given. Since Ceawlin lost his throne in the year of the battle and not in the year of his death, historians speculate that it was Ceol, the next king of Wessex, who plotted against him. Other scholars prefer to think it was an alliance of the Angles and Britons who had a powerful enough army to challenge *Bretwalda* Ceawlin. There is a possibility that

Wessex was fragmented at this point as well because of the surviving grandsons of Cynric, Ceol and Ceolwulf. It is presumed that the brothers were based in Wiltshire while Ceawlin had his base in the upper Thames Valley. It must have been this split of Wessex that influenced the rise of King Ethelberht of Kent.

Even after Ceawlin's death, Wessex continued to be a military power, as there is evidence of successful battles against Essex and Sussex approximately twenty years after his death.

Dynastic Turmoil, Acceptance of Christianity, and the Rise of Mercia

The next king of Wessex was Ceol, who was most likely Ceawlin's nephew, and he reigned from 592 until 597. Ceawlin had a son who should have succeeded him, Cuthwine. However, the fact that Ceol took the throne in the same year as the Battle of Woden's Barrow speaks in favor of the theory that there was a dynastic struggle for power. Cuthwine joined his father in exile after the battle, and it is believed that during the short reign of Ceol, he lived as an outlaw. However, when Ceol's brother, Ceolwulf, took the throne, Cuthwine based his family in the upper Thames Valley, deepening the fragmentation of Wessex. It is believed that the strong families of Devon and Gloucestershire also contributed to the fragmentation as their leaders didn't want to bow to Ceol's rule.

Cuthwine lived a long life, and he must have been a powerful figure during the reign of Cynegils, the son of Ceol, and then Cenwealh, the son of Cynegils. Cuthwine was present at the negotiations with King Penda of Mercia, who, together with his sons, overran the kingdom in 645. However, nothing else is known about Prince Cuthwine except that after the line of Ceol ended in 685, it was his descendants who took the throne.

In 611, Ceolwulf was succeeded by Cynegils, who ruled for 31 years, according to the *Anglo-Saxon Chronicle*. It is possible that by 614, he shared the rule with a certain Cwichelm, but some prefer to think Cwichelm was his son. Bede mentions Cwichelm as the king of Wessex who ordered the assassination of Edwin of Deira in 626. Even though the *Chronicle* gives the impression that Wessex was always ruled by one king, it is quite possible that they often shared the rule with other powerful representatives of the royal family. Whatever their connection was, both Cynegils and Cwichelm fought Penda of Mercia in the Battle of Cirencester in 628, which they lost. Penda took the territories of the Severn Valley and the Kingdom of Hwicce, which had been in the Gewisse's control since Ceawlin took them from the Britons in 577. Cwichelm was last mentioned in the *Chronicle* when he was baptized in 636, as he died the same year.

Cynegils was baptized even earlier in 630 by Bishop Birinus, who established his bishopric at Dorchester. King Oswald of Northumbria acted as a godfather to both Cynegils and Cwichelm. Cynegils's baptism was the first conversion to Christianity ever recorded by a West Saxon king. However, Christianity did not yet spread throughout all the territories of Wessex. In fact, Cynegils's son, Cenwealh, wasn't baptized until much later, after he took the throne in 642. Nevertheless, Wessex was now officially a Christian kingdom, even though the people remained pagan for some time. It is possible that Cynegils agreed to convert in order to form an alliance with the king of Northumbria, Oswald, who married Cynegils's daughter after the king of Wessex was baptized. This alliance was needed to fend off Penda, the king of Mercia, who had already taken some of the territories that belonged to the West Saxons.

Penda's attacks marked the beginning of Mercia's expansion, and the constant pressure they placed on the northern territories of Wessex made its king look to the south for aid. Cenwealh, who succeeded his father in 642, married Penda's sister (or daughter according to other sources), probably intending to repair the relations with the Mercians. Bede tells us that at this time, Cenwealh was still a pagan, and he abandoned his wife so he could take another woman. This angered Penda, who attacked Wessex and drove Cenwealh into exile. It was at the court of King Anna of East Anglia, who had taken him in, that Cenwealh was finally baptized.

Cenwealh came back to Wessex and took the throne once more, probably after Penda's death. Even though he didn't manage to return the territories Wessex had been deprived of by the Mercians, he did expand his kingdom at the expense of the Britons by taking Somerset. Penda's successor, Wulfhere, continued the Mercian pressure on Wessex from the north, but Cenwealh moved to the south, where, in Winchester, he opened another bishopric. This means he took the lands that belonged to the Jutes, who were now confined to the Isle of Wight. These lands would later become the heart of the Kingdom of Wessex. Eventually, Wulfhere advanced south as far as the Isle of Wight, taking the Meon Valley from Cenwealh's kingdom.

Cenwealh died in 672, and some sources mention his widow Seaxburh as ruling for one year after her husband's death. However, it is possible that, like previous kings, Cenwealh shared Wessex, and so did the queen. The *Anglo-Saxon Chronicle* tells us of her succession to the throne, but for this period of medieval history, it was almost unheard of for a woman to rule in her own right. She is also the only woman who appears on the regnal list of the *Anglo-Saxon Chronicle*. On the other hand, the account of Bede tells us that after Cenwealh's death, the kingdom was divided by his sub-kings. It is possible that the situation in Wessex was much more complicated than what the *Chronicle* suggests. Some scholars claim that Bede intentionally refused to mention Seaxburh as she was Cenwealh's second wife. From Bede's Christian viewpoint, she was an illegitimate wife; therefore, her claim to the throne was illegal.

By 674, Wessex had a king again. It was Escwine (Æscwine), the descendant of Ceolwulf of Wessex and the grandson of Cynric. Escwine ruled for only two years, but he managed to defeat King Wulfhere of Mercia at Biedanheafde (unknown location). In fact, there is no evidence of who won the battle, but at around the same time, Wulfhere died, and thus, the Mercian grasp over Wessex was broken. Therefore, historians have concluded that Escwine was victorious. It is unknown what happened to Escwine, but after only two years, the throne of Wessex was succeeded by Centwine, during whose rule the fragmented Kingdom of Wessex became united once again.

Centwine ruled between 676 and 685 or possibly 686, but it is believed he wasn't the only king of Wessex at this point in history. The only event recorded in the *Anglo-Saxon Chronicle* that concerns Centwine is the mention of him driving the Britons to the sea. However, another source, the *Carmina Ecclesiastica* by the Bishop of Sherborne Aldhelm from the 8th century, mentions Centwine and the three battles he won. Aldhelm also records that this king of Wessex was a pagan at first but that later he accepted Christianity, as he became a patron of the churches of his territories. Centwine abdicated in order to become a monk and was succeeded by Caedwalla.

Chapter 3 – Caedwalla and Ine

During the late 7th century, Mercia's power was such that they did not pressure Wessex only from the north. In fact, Wulfhere, the successor to Penda, raided Ashdown in East Sussex in 661, and then he did the same to the Isle of Wight. He placed this kingdom and the district of Meonware under the rule of King Ethelwealh (Æthelwealh) of Sussex. To confirm the alliance between Mercia and Sussex, Ethelwealh was baptized with Wulfhere acting as his godfather. He also married a princess of Hwicce, which was a satellite kingdom to Mercia. Wessex was in danger of being surrounded by Mercia and its allies, and it was probably at this time that Cenwealh subdued the Jutes of Hampshire. However, Wessex gained permanent control of the Jutes' territories during the reign of King Caedwalla, who ruled from 685 until 688.

During the 680s, Wessex was bordered on the west with the British Kingdom of Dumnonia (today's Devon and Cornwall). To the north lay Mercia, which dominated all the kingdoms of southern England. To the southeast, Wessex bordered the South Saxons (Sussex), and to the east, there were the East Saxons (Essex). Although the exact borders are not known, this was the image of England during the late 7th century. Wulfhere was succeeded by his brother, Ethelred (Æthelred), who had no great military ambitions when it came to Wessex; however, the West Saxons were not able to retrieve the territories they had lost in the north. At this time, Wessex was fighting both the Mercians and Britons in Somerset, Gloucestershire, and Wiltshire, but they did keep their influence in the west and south in Dorset and Glastonbury, where the West Saxon kings acted as the patrons of their abbeys.

Caedwalla was the son of Coenberht and the grandson of Cedda, who was the son of Prince Cuthwine. Through this line of ancestors, Caedwalla was a direct descendant of Cerdic, the first king of Wessex. However, Caedwalla is an Anglicized version of the British name Cadwallon, which suggests he was of Briton descent. It is quite possible his genealogy was later added by the scribes of the *Anglo-Saxon Chronicle* to explain his appearance in the royal dynasty of Wessex. Caedwalla is first mentioned in the *Life of St Wilfrid*, a hagiography from the 8th century, as an exiled nobleman. The exile of West Saxon kings wasn't uncommon during the late 7th century, especially because the kingdom was often ruled by more than one king, causing a constant dynastical struggle for power. Even during his days of exile, Caedwalla was able to draw people to himself and form an army, with which he defeated the king of Sussex, Ethelwealh. But Caedwalla didn't manage to keep the territories he gained with this victory, for soon he was expelled from Sussex by its ealdormen.

Caedwalla became the king of Wessex in 685, and he only ruled for two or three years. Bede claims Wessex was still ruled by divided sub-kings by the time Caedwalla took the throne; however, the *Chronicle* claims it was his predecessor, Centwine, who managed to unite the kingdom. It is generally believed that Centwine began his rule as one of the sub-kings but managed to impose his superiority very quickly. However, there is evidence of the existence of these sub-kings during the rule of Caedwalla, as he granted lands to one King Bealdred, who ruled the area of Somerset and West Wiltshire. Another possible sub-king during this period was Cenred, who was the father of the future king of Wessex, Ine. The charters that granted the land to him are dated to 681 and are considered genuine, confirming that Wessex was indeed still divided.

Even though he only ruled for two, possibly three, years, Caedwalla was a very energetic and active king. As soon as he took the throne, he attacked the South Saxons, killing Berthun, one of the ealdormen who drove him out of the territories of Sussex in his first attempt to claim them. Immediately after, Caedwalla conquered the Kingdom of Wight, which was still a pagan territory controlled by Sussex. Caedwalla committed genocide here, as he intended to resettle the island with his own people. In doing so, he killed nearly every native of the island, and even though the heirs of the Kingdom of Wight fled, Caedwalla managed to find them at Stoneham in Hampshire and executed them. Bede mentions a priest persuaded Caedwalla to allow the heir of the pagan Kingdom of Wight to be baptized before his execution. Bede also tells us that Caedwalla was wounded during this conflict but recovered enough to abdicate and travel to Rome, where he was baptized by Pope Sergius I on the Saturday before Easter in 689. Seven days later, he died, probably succumbing to his wounds.

There are surviving charters dated to 688 in which Caedwalla grants individuals the lands in the area of Farnham, making it evident that by this point, he controlled Surrey. Considering that he might have been the founder of the monastery at Hoo, north of Rochester, it is possible he attacked and controlled Kent in 686. Later, he installed his brother Mul as the ruler of Kent, but a revolt occurred, and Mul was burned alive, according to the *Anglo-Saxon Chronicle*. Caedwalla was angered, and he attacked Kent once more, but instead of subduing it, he ravaged the land and left it in chaos. There is a possibility he directly ruled Kent, but there is no written evidence to support this claim. Either way, he extracted the amount of 30,000 pence from the people of Kent as a compensation for the death of his brother Mul. It is believed that this was the price for the life of a prince according to the Anglo-Saxon law of wergild, a term that refers to the defined value of each man's life.

Caedwalla was a Christian king, but he wasn't baptized until his pilgrimage to Rome. On his way, Caedwalla stopped in Francia, where he donated money for the building of a church. There is also a record of him visiting the court of King Cunincpert of the Lombards (northern Italy). Caedwalla was often described as a pagan king, but this is not necessarily the truth. He wasn't baptized because he most likely wanted to choose his own date and place for the sacred ritual. He was respectful of the Church, as there are charters in which he grants lands for various religious buildings. In the *Life of St Wilfrid*, it is described that Caedwalla sought this saint to be his personal spiritual guide. As if to confirm that Caedwalla was a Christian king, Bede said he vowed to give a quarter of the Isle of Wight to the Church, and there are two charters in which he grants the land on the island to the Church.

Ine (r. 689–726)

When writing about Ine, Bede tells us he was of royal blood, which means he came from the Wessex royal family and was probably the descendant of the first kings. The *Anglo-Saxon Chronicle* follows his ancestry by saying that he was the son of Cenred and that Cenred was the son of Ceowald. There is no further information beyond that, but it is safe to assume Ine was, indeed, the distant descendant of Cerdic. But his relationship with the previous king, Caedwalla, is a mystery. It would seem that Ine did not take the throne immediately after Caedwalla abdicated in 688. This might indicate there was some dynastical conflict before Ine was crowned in 689. It is very likely that the sub-kings of Wessex fought for dominance, and Ine was the one who won it. There is also strong evidence that Ine ruled together with his father, Cenred, for some time and that his father remained a sub-king after Ine gained authority above them all.

During the reign of Caedwalla, the territories of Wessex expanded in the south, while the northern territories were lost due to the Mercian attacks. We have a clear picture of what Wessex looked like when Ine took over the throne. The upper Thames Valley was still under the rule of the West Saxons except beyond the northern bank of the river. To the west, the kingdom reached the Bristol Channel;

these territories had belonged to Wessex for over a hundred years before Ine. Caedwalla made himself an overlord of all the southern kingdoms, such as the Isle of Wight, Sussex, and Kent. On the eastern border lie the East Saxons, who controlled London.

Caedwalla left Kent in chaos, but Ine made peace with this kingdom. In 694, the king of Kent, Wihtred, paid Ine what the kingdom was owed for the death of Caedwalla's brother, Mul. The territories in the south were under Ine's overlordship for some time. King Nothhelm of the South Saxons was noted in some charters as the kinsman of Ine. It might be that Ine bound himself with the royal line of Sussex through marriage in order to keep the peace in these territories. There is even evidence that the two kings campaigned as allies in 710, which means that Ine had the South Saxons under his control at this point.

At around the same time, Surrey continued to be a problematic territory, as Essex, Wessex, and Mercia all fought for control over it. The diocese in London had ecclesiastical claim over the territories of Surrey, and it appears that this fact created many problems for the three kingdoms. Finally, in 705, Surrey was transferred to the diocese of Winchester, which gave Wessex full control over it. The letters between Bishop Wealdhere of London and Archbishop of Canterbury Brihtwold, written between 704 and 705, prove that the relations between the East Saxons and the West Saxons were tense at this point. The East Saxons sheltered the exiles from Wessex, which angered Ine and caused the conflict. Ine proposed peace under the condition of Essex expelling those exiles. Bede writes that Sussex was under the control of King Ine for some time before an exile ran to Surrey in 722, which caused Ine to attack Sussex once more. This exile was maybe Ealdbert, a rebellious member of the royal family who was killed during Ine's campaign in Sussex.

The *Anglo-Saxon Chronicle* informs us that Ine and his kinsman Nothhelm fought the Kingdom of Dumnonia, which was ruled by King Geraint. He was the last king of the unified Welsh territories, and he was killed in the battle against Wessex in 710. This campaign brought Devon under Ine's control, making the River Tamar a new border with Dumnonia. However, there is some dispute over the control of Devon, as there is evidence that Ine fought the Britons again at the Battle of Hehil in 722, which Wessex lost. The exact location of this battle is still unknown, and there are speculations that claim it could have been at Devon, while other scholars think it could have been Cornwall.

In 715, the Battle of Woden's Barrow took place, in which Ine participated, but it remains unclear whether the battle was between Wessex and Mercia or if the two kingdoms were allied against a common enemy, an unnamed opponent. The result of the battle is also unknown. It could be that this battle was Ine's attempt to regain the old territories beyond the northern bank of the River Thames, and if that was so, he did not succeed. The territories of the southern bank remained under the control of Wessex, though, as we have evidence of charters being issued in 687 that concerns lands being given to the church at Streatley on the Thames and at Basildon.

Ine was married to Ethelburg (Æthelburg), who is considered to be one of the Anglo-Saxon warrior women. She is remembered in history for burning down the Taunton stronghold in 722 while she was attempting to discover where the traitor and rebel Ealdbert was hiding. This incident may speak of some dynastical unrest, as the exile Ealdbert was a part of the royal family. Furthermore, the *Anglo-Saxon Chronicle* records that Ine slew someone named Cynewulf. Nothing is known about this person, but his name does suggest a connection to the royal house of Wessex. If the connection between the two events is proven to be true, it would confirm the theory that Ine faced an internal resistance that had to be dealt with.

Ine was a Christian king as well, and it is interesting that during his reign, the first nunneries were opened in Wessex. This was done by Ine's kinswoman, Edburga, the daughter of King Centwine. The second woman who was a key person for opening places of worship for women was Ine's sister Cuthburh; she founded the abbey of Wimborne. She was married to King Aldfrith of Northumbria, but they separated, after which she returned to her brother's court.

Ine abdicated the throne in 726, leaving no obvious heir. Bede records that Ine left his kingdom to the younger men and went on a journey with his wife Ethelburg to Rome. There, both of them died. In the early medieval period, a pilgrimage to Rome was thought to give one a better chance for admission to heaven. It is possible that Ine founded the Schola Saxonum, a charity institution for all the Saxon pilgrims who came to Rome, in 727, but some historians believe it was Offa of Mercia who actually did so. This institution must have played an important role, as Bede informs us that everyone wanted to go to Rome, whether they were a man or a woman, noble or freeman, young or old.

Ine was succeeded by Ethelheard (Æthelheard), who ruled from 726 to740. He might have been his brother-in-law, but his true ancestry remains unknown. It is even possible Ethelheard was the first king of Wessex who was not a direct descendant of Cynric.

Ine's Law

The first legal codes to survive this period are the ones from 602/603 by King Ethelberht of Kent, as well as ones from the 670s or 680s by Kings Hlothhere and Eadric of Kent. Ine was the first Wessex king whose law survived until today, and it dates from 694, possibly even earlier. At around the same time, Wihtred of Kent issued his law code because the two kings agreed on peace after the payment for the death of Prince Mul. Under these conditions, Ine and Wihtred probably cooperated on creating their laws. The evidence to support this claim is in one clause that is completely identical in the codes of both kingdoms. Another piece of evidence for this collaboration is that the king of Kent often used the term "eorlcund," which is a West Saxon word for noble. This is why both Kentish and Wessex laws are considered to have been issued as a means to reestablish authority in both kingdoms and to promote peace.

Ine's law code did not survive in its original form, and only some small parts of its copies are available today. However, his laws are known to us because Alfred the Great later implemented them in his own code of laws, which were issued during the 9th century. Alfred was careful enough to note which laws in his own code belonged to Ine. There might be some of Ine's laws that are missing, though, as Alfred, in his prologue to his code, wrote that he did not note the clauses of the previous rulers he disliked. As such, we cannot be sure if Alfred's version of Ine's laws is complete since he did not specify what laws he omitted. What Alfred did include in his own code is the prologue to Ine's laws, which includes the advisors who helped the 7th-century Wessex king. These names were Bishop Earconwald, Bishop Hedde (Hædde), and Ine's father, King Cenred.

From the laws themselves, it is clear that Ine intended to promote Christianity. He was a Christian king, and he wrote, for example, that the oath of a Christian is worth more than the one of a non-Christian. He also addresses the rites of baptism and observance, which are not secular issues a king should worry about. But he did write laws that deal with civil issues. For example, all ceorls (freemen) were obliged to fence their land. If one failed to do so, and his cattle wandered to the land of another ceorl, he would be held liable for all the damage his cattle caused. From Ine's legal code, we can also learn that tenants held the land in tenure from the lord, and the relationship between the lord and tenant was in the king's complete control. However, Ine's laws do not deal with the problems of the lords, and they do not offer any solutions for the compliance of the ceorls.

Ine's laws confirm the theory that in Wessex, at least during the 7th century, ceorls practiced an open-field farming system when it came to agriculture. This means that the ceorls had the complete right to the land they rented from their landlords and that the land would be inherited by their descendants. This system of agriculture was widely used throughout medieval Europe, but it seems that not all of Wessex followed it. Devon, for example, was exempted from this law.

Other laws of Ine concern military service and the fines both nobles and ceorls had to pay for avoiding it. This fine was 120 shillings for nobles and 30 shillings for freemen. This law confirms that ceorls were obliged to serve in the army, which was an old Anglo-Saxon practice. Scholars agree that it is logical that the land workers would have had to fight their king's wars, as a defeat in battle could mean going from a freeman to a slave under the new ruler.

There is evidence that before Ine's rule, the laws stated that anyone who was accused of murder must have the support of his kin, who would then swear an oath to clear the accused of the suspicion. Ine changed this law and recorded that anyone accused of murder must have a high-ranking person to swear this oath. Ine's laws favored Anglo-Saxon citizens over the British who lived in Wessex. The price of a Celtic life was half the price of an Anglo-Saxon life. Also, the oaths sworn by the Celts counted less than Anglo-Saxon oaths.

Chapter 4 – Problems in the North

The Rivers Thames and Avon are often seen as the borders between Wessex and Mercia. However, these borders often fluctuated as both kingdoms wanted to control all of the valleys that surrounded the rivers. It is no wonder they couldn't settle on the borders. Rivers and their valleys were an exceptional commodity to the kingdom with their fertile lands and merchant towns. The Thames and Avon were especially significant as they provided the Anglo-Saxon kingdoms with access to the sea and trade beyond Britain. The *Anglo-Saxon Chronicle* gives us the record of some of the most significant battles fought over these areas. However, the most reliable sources are the charters and land grants to the churches. Looking at which king issued the charter shows us under whose rule these territories were. Charters are also often precisely dated, which helps scholars establish a precise timeline for various events.

The borderlands between Wessex and Mercia were often in conflict, and the lands were often too devastated by war to fulfill their potential. For example, Malmesbury, which lies on the Wiltshire bank of the River Avon, was controlled by the kings of Wessex, while Bath, right across the river, was controlled by the Mercian satellite kingdom Hwicce. During the 680s, Malmesbury received land grants from both Mercian and Wessex kings. The Mercians did have a custom of providing patronage to the churches in their enemy's lands in the hopes that they would attract the people to their side. It seems that Malmesbury profited from both sides, though, as the abbey lay on the border. But it seems that the danger of constant war was greater than the benefits, as the Abbot of Malmesbury, Aldhelm, wrote to Pope Sergius I to plead to both Ine of Wessex and Ethelred of Mercia to agree that his abbey would not suffer during their wars.

The upper Thames Valley was the heartland of the Gewisse territory; it was actually where their first settlements were erected. However, this is also the territory they first lost to the Mercians during the 7th century, and it is hard to pinpoint where the new border with the north was. Many scholars suggest Ashdown to be the most objective marker for the border during this period in the Middle Ages. Ine possibly recovered control of Berkshire all the way to the Thames River, but this was based on a wrong reading of the charter, which supposedly granted the lands to the Abingdon Abbey. The current reading of the document suggests the charter did not concern this abbey but rather the minister at Bradfield in South Berkshire. The battle Ine fought at Woden's Barrow against or in an alliance with Mercia might have been for the control of the Vale of the White Horse, the area in between the Thames and the North Wessex Downs.

After the death of Ine, the situation on the northern borders didn't settle. King Ethelbald (Æthelbald) of Mercia invaded Wessex in the heartlands of Somerset in 733. It was this invasion that established Mercian overlordship over the West Saxons and their king Ethelheard (r. 726-740). Cuthred of Wessex (r. 740-756) was obliged to follow the Mercian king in an attempt to subdue Wales. The strongest evidence of Ethelbald ruling over Wessex at this point is the charters in which he, in his own right, granted the lands of Wessex to others. During the early 750s, Cuthred tried to gain independence for Wessex, and although he succeeded, he only managed to hold onto it until the end of his reign. Cynewulf, who became the king of Wessex in 757, was a witness to the charters of Ethelbald, who granted the lands of Tockenham to Malmesbury. Cuthred's reign was a time of turmoil for Wessex, as Ethelbald of Mercia persuaded Prince Cynric, Cuthred's son, to try to dispose of his father. Cynric was killed during this attempt, and it wasn't long before Ealdorman Ethelhun (Æthelhun) raised a rebellion against Cuthred. However, this rebellion was over before 752 when Cuthred gained Ethelhun's trust, and together, they brought independence to Wessex.

Ethelbald of Mercia was murdered in 757, and Cynewulf took advantage of Mercia's dynastic struggle to retrieve territories in northern Wessex. He also annexed some lands of Hwicce, a kingdom that was undergoing the process of complete absorption into Mercia. Cynewulf issued charters in which he granted the lands north of the Avon to Bath, which suggests he was trying to establish his authority over the area of Hwicce. But the dynastic trouble in Mercia didn't last long, and it resulted in Offa taking the throne, who proved to be one of the greatest Mercian kings.

Cynewulf was now facing a dangerous enemy, and in 779, they fought the Battle of Bensington, where the king of Wessex was defeated and forced to give back the territories of Hwicce. Eventually, Offa of Mercia ruled all of the Midlands, and he imposed his overlordship over all of the southern states. He is regarded as the most powerful Anglo-Saxon king that ruled before Alfred the Great.

In 786, the Wessex throne was succeeded by Beorhtric (r. 786-802), probably with the help of Offa, whom he accepted as the overlord of Wessex. Together, the Wessex and Mercian kings ruled, but it was Offa who granted the charters in the borderlands to the north, which implies he took direct control of these territories. Beorhtric married Offa's daughter Eadburg, who is said to have had more power and ruled instead of her husband. She ordered the executions of her enemies in her own name, and even if her husband King Beorhtric didn't agree, she would use poison to get rid of the people she considered dangerous to their rule. Asser, the 9th-century biographer of Alfred the Great, records that Queen Eadburg accidentally poisoned her own husband and was exiled to Francia by King Ecgberht, the successor to the throne of Wessex. She took refuge at the court of Charlemagne, the ruler of the Western Roman Empire, and it was there, in Francia, that she became an abbess. However, Eadburg was accused of fornicating with another Saxon man and was expelled from the monastery. Charlemagne left her on the streets, and she ended her life as a beggar.

Even though Beorhtric was the Mercian puppet king, he used his influence to gain some possessions in the northern border territories. An estate at Purton was given to him, which he restored to Malmesbury. However, he also agreed to give the Glastonbury Abbey to a member of the Mercian royal house, Cynehelm. Berkshire also stayed under Mercian rule, and Offa made sure to pass the family monasteries in the borderlands to the members of his royal family. In this way, Cookham became the possession of his widow, Cynethryth.

After the death of Beorhtric in 802, Ecgberht was crowned as the new king of Wessex. Immediately, he became involved in a war that occurred between Hwicce and Wiltshire. After a decisive battle, North Wiltshire and Somerset were finally recognized as a part of the Kingdom of Wessex. Even though there is no record of Glastonbury officially being part of Wessex at this point, there is no more mention of its monastery belonging to the Mercian royal family. The northern border of Wessex was restored to its previous shape in the late 7th century. Bath and its monastery remained in Mercia's possession, while Malmesbury remained a part of Wessex. However, from this point on, at the beginning of the 800s, Wessex started its expansion, while Mercia was facing the beginning of its decline. However, the conflict in the north was far from over.

Chapter 5 – The Expansion of West Saxon Power

Ecgberht (r. 802–839)

It is hard to trace the genealogy of Ecgberht as it varies depending on what version of the *Anglo-Saxon Chronicle* you look at. The oldest version, known as the *Parker Chronicle*, is what historians take as being the closest to the truth. According to this version, Ecgberht was the son of Ealhmund of Kent, and through him, he was the descendant of the unknown Eoppa and Eafa, who were the sons of Ingild, the brother to King Ine of Wessex. The genealogy continues further to Cerdic, the founder of the Wessex dynasty. However, this genealogy is often disputed; it is thought that the claims he was of Kentish origin and that his connection to the Wessex royal family were manufactured to create legitimacy for his rule.

If Ecgberht was of Kentish origins, it is quite possible he was forced to run to Wessex when he was very young, as Offa of Mercia subdued Kent and even possibly annexed it during the late 780s. Ecgberht would have remained a threat to Offa as he was the rightful heir to the Kentish throne. Ecgberht tried to take over the throne of Wessex after the death of Cynewulf in 786; however, he was defeated by Beorhtric, who most likely had Offa's help. Ecgberht was forced to live in exile, and he took refuge at the court of Charlemagne in Francia for the next three years. It is possible that instead of spending only three years in exile, he spent thirteen, and the first number might have been an error in the *Anglo-Saxon Chronicle*. Beorhtric ruled for sixteen years, and it is very unlikely Ecgberht would have been allowed to return to Britain during that time.

Charlemagne may have even helped Ecgberht win the throne of Wessex once Beorhtric died in 802. Some even speculate he had the help of the pope himself, but there is not much evidence to support this, except the fact that the pope always supported Charlemagne. The Mercians continued to oppose Ecgberht, and the Kingdom of Hwicce attacked the Wessex territories of Wiltshire on the very day of Ecgberht's accession. The Wessex ealdorman of Wiltshire was victorious, though, and there is no further record of Ecgberht's relations with Mercia for the next twenty years. There is also no evidence that he ever submitted to Mercian rule, and it is quite likely Ecgberht had no influence beyond the borders of his kingdom. It is generally believed that Ecgberht maintained the independence of Wessex but couldn't impose his overlordship on the southern kingdoms. During the next few years, Ecgberht focused on his campaigns with the Welsh, and in 815, he ravaged the lands of Dumnonia (Cornwall), where he would return on a second campaign ten years later.

One of the most important battles in the history of the Anglo-Saxon kingdoms took place during the reign of Ecgberht of Wessex. The Battle of Ellandun (also spelled as Ellendun) took place in 825, where Beornwulf of Mercia was defeated by the king of Wessex. The importance of this battle lies in the fact that after this defeat, Mercia's supremacy over the southern kingdoms started its decline. The place of the battle is recognized to be today's Wroughton in Swindon. The *Anglo-Saxon Chronicle* gives us a description of the battle, and it records that Ecgberht sent his son Ethelwulf (Æthelwulf) to lead the armies of Wessex against Baldred of Kent. Ethelwulf defeated Baldred, and the *Chronicle* records that at this point, all the men of Kent, Sussex, and Essex bowed to Ethelwulf. Here, the *Chronicle* gives a comment that the people recognized they had been wrongfully divided from their Wessex relatives. This passage probably refers to King Offa of Mercia, as he had annexed Kent before Ecgberht's rule during the 780s. The *Anglo-Saxon Chronicle* doesn't give detail who was the aggressor in the Battle of Ellandun, but historians agree that it must have been Beornwulf, who took the advantage to attack during Ecgberht's campaign in Wessex that same year. It is possible the threat of unrest in the southern kingdoms motivated Beornwulf to attack and try to secure Mercia's dominance in the southern territories.

After this battle, Mercia lost its power in the south; however, this wasn't the only consequence of the Battle of Ellandun. The following year, East Anglia asked Ecgberht for protection against Mercia, as Beornwulf had attacked them with the intention to recover his overlordship of that Anglo-Saxon kingdom. Beornwulf died in this attempt, and so did his successor, Ludeca, who attempted an attack on East Anglia a year later in 827. Mercia couldn't foresee the outcome in East Anglia, and instead of reaffirming their dominance, they lost it all to Wessex. It was Ecgberht now who was the dominant power in the southeast and who was the real threat to Mercia.

Ecgberht moved fast, and in 829, he invaded Mercia, which was ruled by Wiglaf at the time. He drove the Mercian king into exile and took control of London, where he issued his own coins as the direct ruler of Mercia. Once Ecgberht took control of Mercia, he was referred to as a *bretwalda* in the *Anglo-Saxon Chronicle*. Ecgberht was the eighth *bretwalda* in the history of the Anglo-Saxon kingdoms, and he only appears in the *Chronicle*. This is because Bede died in 735 before Ecgberht's rule, and thus only lists seven. In the same year, the king of Northumbria, Eanred, submitted to the rule of Wessex. It is likely that Northumbria didn't submit of their free will, as the later chronicler Roger of Wendover from the 12th century notes that Ecgberht raided the country before they submitted. However, the

Chronicle doesn't mention these events, and it is unknown which source Roger of Wendover used in his writings.

Only a year after the invasion, in 830, Mercia regained its independence, as Wiglaf managed to take the throne once more. There are no recorded events that would explain how Wiglaf managed to regain his kingdom, but it was most likely due to the rebellion of the Mercian nobles against the rule of Wessex. It is also possible that, at the same time, East Anglia regained its independence, as its king, Ethelstan (also spelled as Athelstan or Æthelstan), minted his own coins during this period. It seems that after Wessex had its sudden rise to power during the 820s, it could not keep the acquired territories under its control. Historians have tried to understand the reason behind this failure, and one of the proposed theories is that it was the support of the Carolingians that helped Wessex climb to overlordship and that the lack of their assistance must have caused the downfall of Wessex. The most probable reason for the lack of support during the 830s is the rebellion that happened in Francia against their king, Louis the Pious, due to the collapse of the trade network of the kingdom. Once the Carolingians stopped meddling in the politics of Britain, Mercia, Wessex, and East Anglia had to find a balance of power on their own.

However, Wessex did manage to change the geopolitical scene of Anglo-Saxon England as it managed to gain control of the southeastern kingdoms. Essex probably remained under Mercia's control, but East Anglia managed to finally gain its independence. Ecgberht annexed Sussex and Kent into Wessex, and they never gained independence again. At first, they operated as sub-kingdoms of Wessex, but soon enough, they were fully integrated. However, Mercia remained a constant threat to Wessex, and to counter its influence over the northern border territories, Ethelwulf, the son of Ecgberht, issued charters in which he granted the lands and estates to Canterbury Christ Church.

It was during the reign of Ecgberht of Wessex that the Vikings attacked, and the kingdom was defeated by the Danes in 836 in the Battle of Carhampton. The Danes allied themselves with the Western Welsh people, but Ecgberht managed to win a victory in 838 at the Battle of Hingston Down in Cornwall and regain the territories that had been previously lost. Dumnonia was one of the last British kingdoms that were still independent at this time, but after this battle, it ceased to exist. At this point, the settlement of the Anglo-Saxons in Cornwall began, and even though no written record speaks of this process, some conclusions can be drawn by the names of certain places. The new border was the River Ottery, and all the places south of it remained named in Cornish style, while to the north, most of the places were heavily influenced by the Anglo-Saxon settlers.

Ethelwulf (r. 839–858)

Ecgberht died in 839 and was succeeded by his son, Ethelwulf. However, Ethelwulf had already ruled as a sub-king, as he was appointed to Kent in 825 after the Battle of Ellandun. When Ethelwulf took the throne in 839, his oldest son, Ethelstan, was already old enough to be appointed as king of Kent, and he ruled it until his death in 852. With the crown, Ethelwulf inherited his father's great wealth, which he had acquired during his conquests of Mercia, the southern kingdoms, and Wales. Ecgberht used part of this wealth to secure the Church's support for the accession of his descendants. He bribed the archbishop of Canterbury, and in return, he received a promise that the Church would always support his dynastic line in future struggles for the throne. This implies that Ethelwulf might have had enemies who challenged his succession. However, there is no record of such struggles when it came to be his time to rule.

Ethelwulf's reign was modeled by the Carolingian system of family rule, in which each son would be a sub-king to his father, who was superior over them all. In this tradition, Ethelwulf gave the kingdoms of Kent, Sussex, Essex, and Surrey to his sons when they came of age. However, sub-kings did not have the power to issue charters of their own; they were only allowed to witness Ethelwulf's. He allowed his sons to become witnesses as young as six years old. To secure the support of the local nobles, he appointed them as ealdormen of their respective kingdoms. He chose only Kentish nobles to act as the earls of Kent, the nobles of Sussex areas were the earls of Sussex, and so on. Ethelwulf also gained the ealdormen's support by paying them enough respect, sometimes even ranking them higher in the witness lists than his own sons who were sub-kings.

Ethelwulf showed a friendly face to Mercia, and instead of trying to invade its territories, he offered an alliance against their common enemy, the Vikings. The friendship between the two Anglo-Saxon kingdoms was firm enough for Wessex to help King Beorhtwulf of Mercia to issue his own coins. Ethelwulf allowed the Mercians to produce their coins using the same die-cutters that were used for the minted Wessex coins. Although Wessex coins were issued in Rochester, the same craftsmen issued them for Mercia in London. Further proof of the alliance through these coins comes from the fact that Mercian coinage had the same design on the reverse side as the Wessex coins had on their obverse. However, some speculate that instead of being a sign of the alliance, the similarity between the coins might have been the sign of a forgery or an unskilled craftsman who simply reused Ethelwulf's design.

The alliance of the two kingdoms survived the death of Beorhtwulf and continued during the reign of his successor, Burgred. Ethelwulf helped Burgred regain Mercian control over the Welsh territories, and in 853, he married his daughter, Ethelswith (Æthelswith), to Burgred. Sometime before this, some of the Mercian territories passed under the rule of Wessex, but the circumstances are unrecorded. By 844, Berkshire was still a Mercian territory, but it eventually became a part of Wessex, as Alfred the Great, the son of Ethelwulf, was born on the royal estate of Wantage in Berkshire in 849. This estate wouldn't be considered royal if the territory did not pass to Wessex. However, Ethelwulf continued his practice of appointing local ealdormen in the newly acquired Mercian territories, probably to gain their support and manage the peace.

Ethelwulf decided to go on a pilgrimage to Rome in the 850s at the height of his power. It's speculated that before his departure, he gifted a tenth of his wealth to his subjects. However, there are various charters issued in different years that mention this "decimation" of the kingdom, and since none of them are original, some scholars believe they are frauds. However, the biographer of King Alfred, Asser, mentions the decimation too, and he dates it happening in the year 855. It might be that Asser simply translated what the *Anglo-Saxon Chronicle* recorded about this event and either intentionally chose to translate only some parts or loosely translated it. By all sources, it seems that Ethelwulf left a tenth of his lands to the Church and the people. By people, historians believe he meant tenants, meaning the land was now their personal property. However, it remains uncertain if Ethelwulf did this with his own personal possessions or the land that generally belonged to the kingdom.

By the time Ethelwulf went on his pilgrimage, his sons Ethelbald and Ethelberht were both adults, and so, the king left Wessex in their care. When Ethelwulf departed in 855 for Rome, he brought his youngest son, Alfred, with him. Scholars speculate that since Alfred was the youngest, he was chosen to accompany his father as he was intended for a role in the Church. Another theory is that Ethelwulf chose to bring his youngest son to be affirmed by the pope as throne-worthy. Alfred claimed that Pope Leo IV confirmed him as a possible heir to his father, though historians believe this claim might be propaganda to legitimize his rule over his brother's son.

Ethelwulf stayed in Rome for one year, where he gifted the Roman diocese with a gold crown, two golden goblets, a sword decorated with gold, four silver bowls, two silk tunics, and two veils woven with gold. He also gifted gold to the clergy and silver coins to the people of Rome. Ethelwulf's gifts were rich enough to rival the gifts of the continental kingdoms, as he was showing off the generosity and spirituality of Wessex. Historians agree that Ethelwulf's pilgrimage is very strange. No other medieval king felt safe enough to leave his kingdom for such a long period and hoped to return without facing any problems. Even more odd is the fact that Wessex wasn't safe at all at this time due to the constant Viking threat. The only explanation scholars found for Ethelwulf's pilgrimage is that maybe he was driven by his religious views. Maybe he considered this pilgrimage was needed to placate God's wrath, who had sent the Vikings to punish England for its sins.

On his way back to Wessex, Ethelwulf stayed with the Frankish king, Charles the Bald, and there he married his daughter Judith, who was only twelve or thirteen at the time. All of his sons were by his previous wife, and he had no children with Judith. This marriage was strange, even to the contemporaries of King Ethelwulf, for three reasons. First, Frankish princesses were almost never married to foreigners; they were more often sent to nunneries instead. Secondly, Judith was anointed as a queen. This practice was reserved for the empresses of the Western Roman Empire, and Judith was the first queen to be anointed. The third reason lies in the Wessex custom of not allowing queens to rule. The king's former wife in Wessex never had the title of a queen, and she never ruled as an equal to her husband. She was simply the king's wife and nothing more.

Upon his arrival in Wessex, Ethelwulf had to face the revolt of his second son Ethelbald, who did not want to allow his father to recover the throne. The reason for this, according to historians, is Ethelwulf's marriage to the Frankish princess. It is possible that her anointment meant that at least part of Wessex would be inherited by her sons, and this must have sparked Ethelbald's resentment toward his father. The rebellion ended with Ethelwulf agreeing to part with Kent and allowing his son Ethelberht to rule as its rightful king, while Ethelbald became the co-ruler of Wessex. It may be that Ethelwulf agreed to this because he was afraid that a civil war could ignite and divide the kingdom even more.

Ethelwulf died on January 13th, 858. The division of his kingdom continued after his death, as was intended. Ethelbald ruled Wessex, while his brother, Ethelberht, ruled Kent and the territories to the southeast. Queen Judith brought great prestige to the kingdom as a Frankish princess, and in order not to lose it, Ethelbald married her, to the horror of the Church as she was his step-mother.

After Ethelbald died, which happened only two years after his father's death, Judith sold her possessions and returned to her father's court in Francia. There, she met Baldwin I, Count of Flanders, but Charles the Bald wouldn't allow her to marry him. The couple escaped to the north with the help of Judith's brother, Louis, the heir to the Frankish throne. Charles was so angry that he had his bishops excommunicate the couple and forbade any kingdom to shelter them. In response to her father's acts, Judith and Baldwin traveled to Rome, where they persuaded Pope Nicholas I to cancel their excommunication and acknowledge their marriage. Finally, Charles the Bald accepted his daughter's marriage, and the couple had a son, who later married Elfthryth (Ælfthryth), who was Ethelwulf's granddaughter and the youngest daughter of Alfred the Great.

Chapter 6 – The Royal Brothers

Ethelwulf had a will prepared when he died, which left his kingdom divided between his two eldest sons. His will did not survive the ages; however, Alfred's did, and it mentions his father's intent. The kingdom was to pass to whichever of his sons survived, Ethelbald, Ethelred, or Alfred. Ethelberht was exempt as he ruled Kent, and it was presumed his heirs would inherit that kingdom. However, scholars cannot agree if this will was intended for the whole kingdom or the king's personal possessions. Some even claim both, while others argue that it was unlikely for the whole kingdom to be passed down by a will. Some historians argue that if Ethelwulf left the kingdom in his will, it would have definitely lead to fratricide in the dynastic struggle, which did not happen. It is more likely that the brothers made a deal between themselves to pass the throne to each other. But Ethelwulf's movable riches, such as money and horses, were divided between his children and the nobles. In addition, one-tenth of his hereditary land was to be given to the poor for the salvation of the king's soul. In addition, Ethelwulf ordered three hundred gold coins to be sent to Rome each year.

Ethelbald (r. 855–860)

Ethelbald was the second son of Ethelwulf and his first heir, as Ethelwulf's oldest son, Ethelstan, had died in the early 850s. Ethelbald ruled alongside his father for the last two years of his life, although some historians see this arrangement differently. The *Anglo-Saxon*

Chronicle doesn't record what happened in the kingdom after Ethelwulf's return from Rome. The only source of the events we have is Asser's biography of Alfred the Great, and in it, he claims that Ethelwulf divided his kingdom to avoid a civil war. The most common opinion is that Ethelwulf allowed Ethelbald to rule Wessex together with him, while Kent and the eastern provinces of Essex, Sussex, and Surrey were under the rule of his brother Ethelberht. Other scholars don't agree and prefer to think that the division of the kingdom went even further. They believe that Ethelbald kept his power base and court at Selwood while Ethelwulf ruled only the east of the kingdom, and Ethelberht kept Kent. There is even a third opinion that suggests Ethelbald kept the sole rule of Wessex while Ethelwulf took back Kent and the eastern provinces from Ethelberht.

When Ethelwulf died in 858, Ethelbald continued his rule of Wessex as the sole ruler. As mentioned above, Ethelbald married his step-mother, Queen Judith, but the *Anglo-Saxon Chronicle* ignores this marriage and does not record it. Asser condemned this relationship as well, calling it disgraceful to God. By his words, not even the pagans practiced such marriages. It is possible that the *Chronicle* avoids mentioning the marriage because its prestige would cast a shadow over the greatness of Alfred, during whose reign this document was written. However, other than Asser's condemnation, it seems that the marriage wasn't opposed during the reign of Ethelbald. The Frankish *Annals of St Bertin* does mention the marriage but without any comment on its validity. However, it does tell us how, upon her return to the court of Charles the Bald, she was treated with all the honor of a queen.

The first record of Ethelbald survives in the charter of 840, where his name is written in the list of witnesses as *filius regis* (the king's son). He also appears in other charters with the titles *dux filius regis* and sometimes only as *dux* (ealdorman). The *Anglo-Saxon Chronicle* first records Ethelbald when he accompanied his father in the Battle of Aclea, where, together, they defeated the great Viking army.

However, little is known of the period where Ethelbald ruled alone as only two charters have survived. The first one is from 858, and it is a grant of an estate at Farnham to the king by Swithun, the bishop of Winchester, to the king. According to some historians, this means that Ethelbald confiscated the lands of the bishop for his own personal use. The second charter is dated from 860, and it is a grant of land by the king to his thegn (a rank of the aristocracy that fell below ealdorman) named Osmund. Queen Judith was a witness for both of these charters, which had never been practiced before in Wessex since the king's wife had no real power.

Ethelbald died in 860, but the reason for his death is unknown. There is not much left as evidence of his reign, but his reputation suffered due to his rebellion against his father and his marriage to his step-mother. These accusations are first recorded in Asser's writing, and later historians and chroniclers took this stance against him as well. Ethelbald is generally remembered as a weak king who achieved nothing, with Wessex suffering from a period of lawlessness during his reign. It is not known whether he had any children, but if he did, they are not mentioned in any of the sources.

Ethelberht (r. 860–865)

Ethelberht was the third son of King Ethelwulf, and he inherited the throne of Wessex upon his brother's death. He had already ruled Kent and the eastern provinces, and thus, the throne of Wessex allowed him to unite the kingdom once again under one king. His first appearance in the medieval records is in the charter of 854, only a year before his father divided the kingdom before his pilgrimage to Rome. After Ethelwulf's return, Ethelberht continued to reign in Kent, probably as a sub-king. In 858, he became the sole king of Kent, Surrey, Essex, and Sussex by his father's wish.

Once Ethelbald died in 860, Ethelberht succeeded the throne to the Kingdoms of Wessex and Kent. It is possible that Ethelred and Alfred were supposed to inherit the throne of Wessex since Ethelberht had been exempted from his father's will since he already ruled Kent. However, it seems that both of his younger brothers were too young to take the throne, and the crown passed to Ethelberht instead. At this time, Wessex was under the threat of Viking attacks, and it would have been of questionable wisdom to appoint children as its rulers.

Ethelberht refused to appoint a member of his family to rule Kent and the eastern provinces; instead, he chose to unite the kingdoms. It was in the first year of his rule that he issued a charter with witnesses from both Wessex and Kent. This is the first charter of the united kingdom, and as such, it represents a significant point in English history. It contains the names of the archbishops of both Canterbury and Rochester and the names of the bishops of Sherborne, Winchester, Selsey, and London. Ten ealdormen were named from both Wessex and Kent, making this charter unique as it represents the unification of the west and east kingdoms under one rule.

The *Anglo-Saxon Chronicle* tells us that Ethelberht reigned in "harmony and great peace," and it seems that at this point, the brothers agreed that the rule of Wessex should pass among them and not to their sons. The second important charter dates from December 863, in which Ethelberht granted Sherborne Abbey immunity from royal and judicial services. This charter was written in Old English, not in Latin, as was the custom. It could mean that by this time, the transition from Latin to vernacular had already happened, at least when it came to legal documents. Alfred notes that by the time he began his reign, Latin was barely in use anymore.

In the autumn of 865, Ethelberht died and was buried at Sherborne Abbey in Dorset. The cause of death is unknown. Like with his predecessor, there is no record of Ethelberht having any children. Thus, the throne passed to the fourth son of Ethelwulf, Ethelred.

Ethelred I (r. 865–871)

The most notable event of Ethelred's rule must have been when at the Witan (an assembly of nobles and leaders), Alfred asked him to give him his share of the property their father had left to all of his sons when he died. Ethelred answered that he could not divide the property and give Alfred what belonged to him; instead, Ethelred promised he would leave everything to his younger brother after he died. Scholars are still speculating if they were talking about their family's private properties or the whole kingdom. It is possible that Alfred, as the younger brother, wanted to rule Kent and the eastern provinces, as his brothers had during the rule of their father. If this was the case, it is possible Ethelred did not wish to divide the kingdom and make it even more vulnerable to Viking attacks. So, instead, he promised to pass the throne to his younger brother and not to his son. In addition to this argument between the brothers, Alfred rarely shows up as a witness to Ethelred's charters, which might imply they were not in the best relations.

Another important event that occurred during Ethelred's rule is the arrival of the Great Heathen Army in East Anglia. It was at this point that the Viking attacks changed in nature. Instead of just raiding and taking the riches back to their Scandinavian lands, the Danes decided to settle in England. The full invasion of the Anglo-Saxon kingdoms started in the very first year of Ethelred's rule. Although Wessex was not yet directly threatened by this great Viking army, it was just a matter of time. Ethelred tried to help his brother-in-law, Burgred, the king of Mercia, but even together, they were unable to repel the Vikings from Nottingham.

The first attempted invasion of Wessex was in 870 when the Danes took over Reading, a town between the Thames and Kennet Rivers. Ethelred and Alfred were unable to defeat the Vikings there and were forced to flee. But the Danes didn't have their victory over Wessex yet, as both Ethelred and Alfred were still alive and planning a counterattack. Only four days later, their armies met again in battle, and this time, the West Saxons successfully expelled the Vikings out of their kingdom.

Ethelred died in 871 sometime after Easter. The cause of death is not known, but it can be speculated he died of a wound since he fought the Vikings often during the final years of his reign. Asser doesn't reveal much about his death as he only records that Ethelred was a king of a good reputation and that he ruled for five years. Ethelred had two sons who would have probably been able to seize the throne if their father had lived until they reached adulthood. But they were too young to rule, and so, Alfred succeeded his older brother. Alfred would eventually become one of the most famous Anglo-Saxon kings, the only one who was titled "the Great."

Chapter 7 – Alfred the Great
(r. 871–886)

The youngest son of Ethelwulf of Wessex inherited the throne after his three older brothers, Ethelbald, Ethelberht, and Ethelred. During Alfred's life, the Vikings started raiding the coast of England and changed the nature of their attacks from raids to a full-blown invasion. One by one, the Anglo-Saxon kingdoms fell under the rule of the Danes, who intended to settle their population in the newly conquered regions. It was Alfred's Wessex that stood alone, surrounded by the Viking-occupied lands. In fact, it was the last English kingdom to oppose them. Alfred managed to not just preserve Wessex but also to impose his dominance over England. He dared to dream of an England united under a single ruler and for all of the Anglo-Saxon people to bow to him.

Almost everything we know about Alfred's rule comes from his biographer Asser, a scholar and a bishop who is most known for his work titled *The Life of King Alfred.* In it, Alfred is described as a merciful king of a gracious nature. It is no wonder he was given the epithet "the Great"; however, this was only done in the 16th century during the Reformation in England. Alfred remains the only Anglo-Saxon king to bear this title, and he was also the first king of England with this title, with Cnut the Great being the only other one.

Childhood

Asser notes that Alfred was born in 849 at the royal estate called Wantage, located in Berkshire. Today, this location is in Oxford. Asser is the main source of the facts known about Alfred's life; however, he might be wrong about his year of birth. The *Anglo-Saxon Chronicle*, which was also written in Alfred's court by his order, notes that he took the throne when he was 23 years old in 871. This would mean his year of birth would be either 847 or 848. But if that is the case, how is it possible that Asser missed a year, especially when he had the knowledge of his contemporaries available, among them the king himself? It is possible that Asser thought Alfred took the throne during his twenty-third year, meaning he was actually 22. This would explain that one-year difference, or maybe Asser was right, and the *Chronicle* miscalculated the year of his birth.

Aside from his birthdate, there is very little we know about Alfred's childhood. His mother, Osburh, was described by Asser as a very religious and noblewoman. He also informs us Osburh was a daughter of King Ethelwulf's butler, who was named Oslac. However, nothing more is known of this woman except that she witnessed one charter in 868, unlike Ethelwulf's second wife, Judith. Alfred the Great later justified the position of Wessex royal women by bringing up the misconduct of a queen at the beginning of the 9th century. He was probably referring to Eadburg, the daughter of Offa, who married the king of Wessex, Beorhtric, and accidentally poisoned him in 802.

It was very unlikely that Alfred would have ever become a king simply because he had four older brothers. Even his name suggests a different intention for their youngest son. While all four of his brothers are named with the beginning "Ethel" ("Æthel" in Old English), which translates to "noble," Alfred's name begins with "Ælf." This element of the name is unusual for Wessex, but it can be commonly found in East Anglia and Northumbria. It means "elf" or "wise"; therefore, his name can be translated as "elf counsel" or "wise counsel." His name might suggest the intention was for Alfred to finish his schooling and devote his life either to God or to the position of advisor to his brothers. However, this theory about his name might be far-fetched as some scholars believe his parents simply liked the name and that no meaning should be attached to it.

Besides the common skills that were taught to all noble boys, such as riding, fighting, and hunting, Alfred extensively learned writing and English poetry. He was literate in both Old English and Latin and was able to speak and write both languages. Later, during his reign, he founded a school for noble boys at his court. He argued that boys should not stop learning even once they began their military training. Alfred was fond of reading and writing, and his pride was in the constant pursuit of wisdom. He was eager to acquire new skills even later in life, saying that learning is a lifetime activity. It is possible that special attention was given to Alfred's education because he was the youngest child that had no real chance of inheriting the throne and instead would have to spend his life in the service of either God or his brothers. Asser tells us the king had a poor education when he was a child, but this might be untrue and simply propaganda meant to justify the reforms of education Alfred implemented during his reign.

The most significant event of Alfred's childhood is certainly his two visits to Rome. In 853, King Ethelwulf sent his youngest son to Rome. Asser writes that Pope Leo IV consecrated Alfred as a king and that he even stood as a sponsor to his confirmation. This means that Alfred was sent to Rome when he was only four or five years old. In medieval times, this was too tender an age for such long travels, making it quite intriguing that Ethelwulf chose to take Alfred on such a perilous journey. However, Asser's record of Alfred being consecrated in Rome is either a misinterpretation of the events or propaganda that would give legitimacy to Alfred's rule when Ethelred's sons were still alive. What really happened is obvious from the letter Pope Leo IV sent to Ethelwulf, a letter that was preserved by the 12th-century scribes. In this letter, the pope tells Ethelwulf that his son has been decorated as a spiritual son, as was the custom of Rome.

Alfred was received by Pope Leo, who honored the little boy in order to preserve good relations between Rome and the Anglo-Saxon Kingdom of Wessex. Alfred became the Roman consul with the pope as his sponsor and spiritual father. This was hardly a kingly consecration. This office of Roman consulship had ceased to exist by the mid-9th century, and it continued to live only as a prestigious title for noble families, whose support the pope expected. Some scholars believe that since Alfred was of such a young age, he could have been under the impression of a grand ceremony, like the one where he was being anointed as king. Later, when he recalled this event, his memory might have been influenced by this childhood impression. However, it certainly helped him to believe and represent himself as a ruler directly consecrated by the pope, with the full right to rule the kingdom instead of his nephew Ethelwold (Æthelwold), the son of the previous king Ethelred, as Ethelwold did have supporters who wanted him to rule instead of Alfred.

The second time Alfred went to Rome was as an escort to his father two years later. Ethelwulf went on a pilgrimage while he was at the height of his power, which was an unusual thing to do in the medieval period, especially with the Vikings being such a close threat to his kingdom. Nevertheless, Ethelwulf chose to spend a whole year in Rome and took Alfred with him. It is possible that Ethelwulf took young Alfred to help prepare the boy for a life devoted to God. What better place for a child to discover the love for the Church than Rome itself? A boy would find the splendors of a richly decorated city attractive and maybe willingly devote his life to God's path. And, as the youngest son, Alfred was expected to find a different path for himself.

The King

Alfred inherited the throne after his brother Ethelred died in 871. Even though he left two sons behind him, they were too young to become rulers. The agreement between Ethelred and Alfred was that whichever brother would survive would inherit the properties of the other. It is unclear whether the kingship was a part of these properties. Nevertheless, Alfred became the king and faced a Danish invasion as early as his brother's funeral. While he was dealing with the matters of Ethelred's burial ceremony and installing his own royal office, the Danes attacked, probably taking advantage of the king's death. The Saxon army suffered a defeat as their new king was absent. Asser writes of Alfred as a great warrior who won all his battles. But this is far from the truth as another defeat soon followed at Wilton. This time, Alfred was present, but the Danes pressed the young king into agreeing to pay them. The Vikings then left Wessex with the treasures Alfred paid them, and they wintered in London.

Finally, Alfred could rule properly, as the money he gave the Danes bought him five years of peace. He was the most improbable of all the kings. Besides being the youngest of five brothers, of which four were his predecessors, he was also the frailest of them all, as Asser reports he was sick from a young age. In *The Life of King Alfred*, Asser left detailed descriptions of this illness, and according to the symptoms, some modern doctors have come to the conclusion that Alfred suffered either from hemorrhoids or Crohn's disease. The illness was very unpleasant and painful, with no known treatment in the medieval period. It must have been a wonder for the Anglo-Saxon nobles and the people in general that Alfred was able to rule at all.

During the five years of peace, it seems that Alfred turned his attention from the Vikings in the north to the economy of Wessex. He restored the silver content of the Wessex coinage, which was probably done in order to increase the value of taxes he imposed on his subjects. He might have started a military reform at this point, but it certainly wasn't finished, which the renewed Viking attacks in 876 prove. There are only two charters from this period of peace that survived, but it's enough to give us a glimpse at what was Alfred's concern at the time. In 873, he made a gift of land to a thegn named Erdwulf. The same land was sold in 785 to Erdwulf's friend Wighelm, and it was done in the presence of Alfred. The lands in concern were in Kent, and Alfred probably did this to ensure the support of the Kentish thegns.

In 876, a new Viking attack followed, and Alfred was again unable to repel it. Instead, he tried to convince the Danes to leave. He realized it wasn't enough to pay them and expect them to never return. He needed some equivalent of a Christian oath to keep the Vikings away. However, he knew that the Christian oath meant nothing to the pagans, so he had to find an alternative. Both Guthrum, the king of the Danes, and Alfred agreed they should exchange hostages. Even though he was Christian, Alfred agreed to swear an oath on Thor's arm ring, a sacred pagan relic, in the hopes that the Vikings would not break such an oath this time. Asser was ashamed to admit this pagan ritual that his beloved Christian king undertook, and he chose not to mention Thor's arm ring in his biography. Instead, he only notes that Alfred took an oath on the relics Alfred trusted after God. Luckily, the *Anglo-Saxon Chronicle* recorded the events and mentioned the pagan arm ring.

However, Alfred was disappointed once more. The Danes used the excuse of the oath and the hostage exchange to slip away and escape to Exeter, where they spent the winter. Instead of releasing the hostages, they chose to kill them all. It is unknown why the Danes didn't keep their promises. Perhaps they considered it to be unworthy to keep an oath with the Christian. Or perhaps they simply tricked Alfred and didn't hold the oath as sacred at all. The truth is, there is little evidence of pagan rituals and beliefs among the Danes who came to England, and the little we know is from the writings of sagas from the 13th century. In any event, the effort Alfred invested in finding common ground with the Danes was a failure.

Alfred's Reforms

Alfred wasn't successful in repelling the Vikings from Wessex until 878. It was evident that he could not continue with the old military system of the Anglo-Saxons if he was to win. The strategies of the Viking armies were completely different, and the Anglo-Saxons were no match for the Danes, who had been brought up in a warrior culture that placed emphasis on raiding. While the Anglo-Saxons attacked by advancing the shield wall toward their enemies head-on, the Danes usually sent smaller groups of attackers from their base, which they could always retreat to if the need arose. The Danes also sought weak points in the Anglo-Saxon shield walls and attacked at those points, which would break it. Also, the Danes were very good at enduring a siege, and it seemed they always had the advantage of provisions, as they prepared their bases well in advance.

The Anglo-Saxons were used to open battle where the king would call on the national militia to defend the kingdom or invade an enemy's lands. But the Danes used a strategy involving hit-and-run tactics. They would send smaller parties to raid and plunder, and the king was unable to predict when and where the next attack would be. Therefore, the king was not able to call all the forces at his disposal and to gather all the needed supplies to fend off the Viking raids. As the locals were unable to deal with the raids by themselves, they often deserted King Alfred and conspired with Guthrum. Alfred learned the lessons from his defeats, and immediately after the victory at Edington in 878, he took the opportunity of peace to reorganize his army.

The central piece of Alfred's military reform was the burhs, which were fortifications and fortified settlements that spread throughout the kingdom like a net of strategically important places. Alfred organized 33 burhs spread apart about 30 kilometers (19 miles). This way, the army was able to confront an attack wherever it came from. Alfred invested in building the walls around the towns, digging defensive dikes, and even reinforcing the wooden palisades. Some old Roman towns, such as Winchester, already had walls, but they were in dire need of repair. Each burh was to be supplied by the landowners of the area. The Burghal Hidage, a contemporary document which describes in detail this system of burhs, survived, meaning we have an insight into how Alfred's military lived and worked. Since the Vikings were famous for their naval force, Alfred built twin-burhs, or twin towns, on each bank of a river. These were connected with a fortified bridge, which also had the role of blocking the river pathway for the Viking ships. The Vikings were not used to besieging, and so, they lacked the equipment to do so. This is why Alfred's system of burhs had an advantage when it came to defense.

Alfred also improved the navy of Wessex with the new designs of ships, which he ordered in 896. He began the construction of around a dozen longships with sixty oars. This design was double the size of the Viking ships, and the *Anglo-Saxon Chronicle* describes them as swift, steady, and being able to ride through shallow waters. Although there are no remains of Alfred's ships, scholars think Alfred used the Roman design with high sides, which were designed for battle and not navigation. This design was meant for open sea battles, and the ships proved to be too large for the rivers where the Danes attacked the most.

In the area of law, Alfred the Great issued the so-called Doom Book, also known as the Legal Code of Ælfred the Great. He wrote his own laws in this book but also gathered the laws of previous kings that he found suitable. Alfred also included the law code of his predecessor, Ine of Wessex. In the introduction to his legal code, Alfred wrote how he had a council that advised him on how to reform some of the previously existing laws that he found unsatisfying. Among other kings whose laws he used, Alfred mentions by name Offa of Mercia and King Ethelberht of Kent, who was the first Anglo-Saxon king to be converted to Christianity.

The code of law is divided into 120 chapters, a symbolic number, as it is the age at which Moses died. Moses was a big symbol for Alfred's code because he is looked at as the link between divine and human laws. One-fifth of the book is the introduction, which Alfred wrote by himself, and it can be observed as his reflection on Christian laws. He even includes all ten commandments and some chapters from the Book of Exodus. The crimes described in Alfred's code can almost all be compensated with payment to their lord. In fact, the only one that cannot be paid is the betrayal of a lord. Alfred thought of lordship as a sacred bond between God and man. To betray a lord is equal to betraying God in his eyes, and no amount of money can justify that.

Alfred insisted that the officials of his kingdom who had the role of judges had to be literate; if they were literate, then they would easily be able to seek out the wisdom needed for their jobs. The disobeying of this act would be punished with the loss of their office. Alfred was a great advocate of education in general, and he is to be thanked for the many religious books that were translated to Old English in order to make them more available to the people.

The Viking raids had had a devastating effect on education in England. One of the reasons for this is that the usual place for learning were the monasteries. And it was the monasteries that were first attacked by the Danes. Many noble houses were reluctant to send their sons to monasteries to learn when there was a danger of losing them due to the raids. The second reason is the constant threat of war that hung above their civilization; due to this danger, there was simply no effort made to promote education, as warriors were in greater need than scholars.

Alfred was aware of all these problems, and he lamented the fate of the education system of England. He wrote about people not being able to read and write contemporary Old English, let alone Latin. He also complained that the quality of the Latin language was dramatically reduced even when used by learned monks who should know better. And from the surviving Latin script, it is observable, even today, the change in the quality of the Latin language, especially in the areas ruled by the Danes, such as East Anglia and Mercia. Wessex still used Old Latin, and it is the kingdom where this ancient language lingered the longest.

Alfred wanted to bring education to the people, and so, he ordered the translation of many "books of wisdom." It is unknown when exactly Alfred ordered this program of translation, but the many books he thought were necessary for all of mankind to understand were translated into Old English. Some he even translated himself, taking great pride in the venture. Among these books were Bede's *Historia ecclesiastica gentis Anglorum* (the "Ecclesiastical History of the English People") and Orosius's *Historiarum Adversum Paganos Libri VII* ("Seven Books of History Against the Pagans").

Alfred also opened a court school in which his own children were to be educated. However, he still allowed the admittance of children of nobles and others of lesser birth. Such a thing had only been done by Charlemagne, who Alfred greatly respected. In court school, the children learned English and Latin, both writing and reading. Alfred recruited scholars from both England and the continent to teach in his court school. The most famous among the Frankish scholars were Grimbald and John the Saxon, while from England, Alfred employed Werwulf from Mercia and Asser from Wales.

The Death and Legacy of Alfred the Great

It is unknown how Alfred the Great died, but the *Anglo-Saxon Chronicle* records it was on October 26th, 899, and by the time of his death, he was fifty years old. It is possible that he died of the illness that had tortured him from a young age. As mentioned before, it was highly likely that Alfred suffered from Crohn's disease, an illness that affects the immune system. This disease occurs in people with a genetic predisposition to it, and it is known that Alfred's grandson, King Eadred, suffered from a similar disease.

Alfred was buried in the Old Minster in Winchester, and from there, his remains were moved to the New Minster and then, in turn, moved to Hyde in 1110. He was buried next to his wife and children. During the 16th century, the Hyde Abbey was destroyed, but the graves remained intact, at least according to the record. It was in the 19th century, during the building of a prison on the same site, that the graves were destroyed and lost. Archeological excavations in 1999 found one pelvis bone, which radiocarbon dating placed as belonging to the correct period of time of Alfred the Great. However, scholars cannot be sure if the bone belonged to Alfred, his son Edward the Elder, or someone completely unknown whose remains happened to be in the same spot.

Alfred was venerated as a saint by the English Christian tradition. King Henry VI tried to have him canonized by Pope Eugene IV in 1441, but he was unsuccessful. Some Catholic traditions do recognize Saint Alfred, but the modern Roman Catholic Church does not. In the churches of England, Alfred is considered a saint and a great hero, whose image is often depicted in stained glass. October 26th is celebrated as a commemorative day in his honor, and it's a feast day.

Alfred is still seen as a pious Christian king, the first to promote the English language instead of Latin, and who started the system of translations in order to make education approachable for the common people. Because of his great desire to spread education all over his kingdom, many educational establishments still carry his name. One such example is Alfred University in New York, which even has its local telephone exchange as 871 in commemoration of Alfred's ascension to the throne. His birthplace of Wantage, Oxfordshire, opened King Alfred's Academy. Because it was believed for many years that Alfred's reform of the English navy was, in fact, the first navy in the territory of Britain, some ships have been named after this king, such as the HMS *King Alfred* under the Royal Navy and the USS *Alfred* under the US Navy.

Chapter 8 – The Great Heathen Army

Viking raids on the territories of Britain started as early as the late 8th century. They were mostly hit-and-run types of attacks focused on monasteries. Their goal was to gather riches and slaves and take them back to their respective countries. However, something drastically changed during the mid-9th century, as the nature of the Viking attacks changed from raids to invasions. It is possible that the sandy Danish land was not fertile enough to grow food for the rising population, causing families to search for new territories that they could inhabit and where they could support themselves through agriculture. These attacks were not happening just in Britain. Some Vikings decided to attack the shores of Normandy. However, the great Danish army landed on the shores of East Anglia. This army was named the Great Heathen Army by the scribes of the *Anglo-Saxon Chronicle*, men who had firsthand experience in facing the invasion.

The army, although sometimes referred to as the great Danish army, didn't consist only of Danes. In fact, it was a coalition of Scandinavian armies, which included Norwegians and Swedes. Due to the mountainous terrain of their countries, which was unsuitable for agriculture, the Norwegian and Swedish Vikings joined their relatives, the Danes, in the invasion of Britain. It was this unified coalition that landed on the shores of England in 865, during the reign of Ethelred of Wessex, Edmund of East Anglia, Ella (Ælla) of Northumbria, and Burgred of Mercia. Kent and Sussex were already a part of Wessex by this time; therefore, they were under the rule of the West Saxon king.

It is unknown what the size of the Viking army was like, as the *Anglo-Saxon Chronicle* uses the term *here*, which is often translated as warband, instead of *fyrd*, meaning army. King Ine of Wessex specified in his law code in 694 that a *here* numbered more than 35 men. It is possible that this term was used more widely during the 9th century and that it was used to differentiate the Viking army from the royal military of the English Crown. Some scholars propose the size of the army was around one thousand men, while others think the number was far greater and that the army consisted of several thousand men. However, if this is true, then we have yet to discover the evidence of the structures that provisioned such a great foreign army in the territory of Britain.

Whatever the truth is about the size of the army, scholars agree on one thing. The Vikings had a custom of joining the warbands of multiple leaders when they had a common cause. These bands would split apart once their task was achieved and the riches were gathered. It is possible that the same happened here and that the Great Heathen Army had more than one leader. The joint armies must have not only consisted of the Vikings from Scandinavia but also the Vikings from Ireland and those who had raided Francia over the past few decades. It is in Francia where the Vikings had discovered how easily the rivers were navigable, which made the inland monasteries and estates vulnerable to attacks. This same tactic was used in the invasion of England. However, the Frankish lords responded by barricading the rivers, making them difficult to raid and causing the Vikings to turn their attention to England.

Legend has it that the leaders of the Great Heathen Army were none other than the sons of Ragnar Lodbrok (also spelled as Lothbrok)—Halfdan Ragnarsson, Ivar the Boneless, and Ubba. The sagas of the north claim that the invasion was launched by the three brothers in order to avenge the death of their father, who had been killed by Ella of Northumbria. However, there is no historical evidence that this ever occurred as history has no evidence that the Norse hero Ragnar ever existed.

The Fall of East Anglia, Northumbria, and Mercia

The Vikings attacked Wessex in 851, and King Ethelwulf defeated them. It must have been a great blow to the Vikings, as they did not want to risk the might and wrath of Wessex again. Instead, they decided to invade England through East Anglia. There, the Danes received horses and payments in exchange for peace. Supplied by the East Anglians, the Vikings turned their attention to Northumbria and York, where they landed their first attack in the autumn of 866. Northumbria was in the middle of a dynastic struggle when the Vikings arrived. The people had disposed of their old king, Osberht, and passed the title to Ella, who was described in later sources as the king's brother. However, there are no contemporary sources to claim this relationship between the two kings. The Viking attack caught Northumbria by surprise, and both claimants to the throne were killed. It was the Vikings who appointed the next king of Northumbria, the puppet ruler Ecgberht. It is not known if he ruled the whole kingdom or just a part of it with the Danes claiming the rest.

Once Northumbria was secured, the Vikings turned back to East Anglia, with which they already had a peace agreement. The first renewed attack against the Anglo-Saxon kingdom happened in the winter of 869 when the Viking army rode through Mercia to reach East Anglia and took Thetford, where they wintered. Almost nothing is known of the rule of King Edmund of East Anglia since the Vikings destroyed all the contemporary evidence. It is just known that he fought the Danes in a battle and lost. He was probably killed during this battle, but the legend of his martyrdom remains. By tradition, the leaders of the Viking army were Ivar and Ubba, and they tortured King Edmund in an attempt to make him renounce Christianity. But Edmund resisted the beating and was finally shot full of arrows. His head was severed from his body and thrown in the woods. According to a legend, the East Anglians found the head by following an ethereal wolf who spoke the Latin words "Hic, hic, hic" (here, here, here) while leading the men to the king's head.

The fall of East Anglia is the first event that the *Anglo-Saxon Chronicle* mentions related to the Viking invasion. Even though Edmund offered horses and paid the Vikings when they first landed on the shores of East Anglia, he was proclaimed a saint almost immediately after his death because he was killed by pagans. At the end of the 9th century, there were even coins issued that had the inscription "sce eadmund rex" (O, Saint, and King Edmund).

The next to be targeted by the Viking army was Mercia, and it came under attack in the autumn of 867. The Viking army conquered Nottingham and decided to spend the winter there. King Burgred of Mercia was married to Ethelswith, the daughter of Ethelwulf of Wessex and the sister to Ethelred and Alfred. Facing the Vikings, he called his brothers-in-law to help him expel them from Nottingham. Ethelred and Alfred came with their armies and laid siege to Nottingham but were unable to draw the Danes out of the city into open conflict. The well-stocked Vikings were able to sit in the city and wait for the siege to break. The Anglo-Saxon army was filled with farmers who, when spring came, had to abandon the siege and go work their farms in order to produce food for the kingdom. Burgred decided to pay the Vikings to leave, and so, Ethelred and Alfred didn't have the chance to battle.

The Vikings came back to Mercia in 874 and drove Burgred out of his kingdom. In his position, they placed Ceolwulf to be their puppet king. Burgred went to Rome after being driven out of his kingdom, where he died. It appears that Ceolwulf did rule without Viking overlordship, at least to some extent, as he issued charters in his own name. And even though the *Anglo-Saxon Chronicle* describes him as the "foolish king's thegn," he was accepted as the ruler by Mercian clergy and nobility, who often witnessed his charters. When the

Vikings came back to Mercia in 877, they divided this kingdom between themselves and Ceolwulf, and he ruled independently in the part of Mercia he had been given until 879. Ceolwulf's Mercia was reduced to the northern and western parts of the previous kingdom. It is possible that the *Chronicle* records Ceolwulf as a thegn in order to strengthen Alfred's claim of overlordship over Mercia. After all, the *Chronicle* was written by his orders at his own court, and it may have been a very biased document.

Wessex and the Vikings

Wessex remained the last Anglo-Saxon kingdom that still resisted the Viking invasion. It was constantly under attacks during the 870s, and at one point, it seemed as if it would be impossible to drive the Vikings out. However, Alfred had brought reform to the military, and the Danes were successfully defeated.

But Alfred wasn't always successful against the Danes. In fact, he lost more battles than he won. As soon as Alfred took the throne, Wessex was attacked by a Viking army, which received reinforcements from the Great Summer Army sent from Scandinavia. This army was led by Bagsecg, a Viking leader whose name was first recorded in the *Anglo-Saxon Chronicle*. The joint army settled at Reading in Berkshire, and from there, they attacked the West Saxon army at an unknown place, where the Saxons lost. In May, at Wilton, Wiltshire, Alfred's army was defeated once more. Alfred was forced to pay the Danes to leave. From Reading, the Viking army continued to Mercia to winter in London, and eventually, they took over that kingdom.

With only one Anglo-Saxon kingdom left, the Vikings returned to Wessex by 876. In the meantime, Ivar the Boneless left the shores of England, and he was never again mentioned in contemporary sources. It is believed he retreated to Ireland to rule the Vikings of Dublin. His departure meant the Great Heathen Army needed a new leader, and Guthrum, who would become known among Christians as Ethelstan, the king of the Danes, was the one to step up to the task. It is not known how Guthrum became the leader of the Danish army, but he was ready to attack Wessex by 876, which was when he led the Danish army from Cambridge into Wessex. Guthrum seized the convent of Wareham in Dorset, where Alfred besieged him. However, Alfred wasn't able to do much, and he once again decided to negotiate for peace. This time, he asked for hostages to be exchanged as a guarantee of their peaceful intentions, and even though Guthrum agreed at first, he broke his promise and slew all the hostages on his way to Exeter, where the Vikings spent the winter. Guthrum expected reinforcements to arrive and join his army at Exeter, but fortune was on Alfred's side. The West Saxon king pursued the Danes and laid another siege at Exeter. This time, Alfred had no reason to negotiate a peace, especially since the Viking reinforcements had wrecked their fleet in a storm. Guthrum finally agreed to release some hostages and leave Wessex, and this time, he kept to his word.

However, Alfred didn't manage to permanently get rid of Guthrum. A year later, in January of 878, the Vikings attacked the royal estate at Chippenham, on the River Avon, where Alfred was spending Christmas. Alfred was unprepared, and the Danes had conquest in mind this time, not loot. Therefore, they pillaged the countryside of Wiltshire, Somerset, and Hampshire, and the king of Wessex was unable to defend his lands. Many landowners chose to submit to the Danes once they realized the royal army was not coming to help them. Among those who surrendered were several ealdormen of Alfred. One of these men was even recorded in a charter that gave his lands away since he had betrayed his king and country.

The *Anglo-Saxon Chronicle* tells us that Guthrum subjected Wessex and its people, except for king Alfred. It is unknown how much of the country Guthrum managed to acquire during this invasion in 878, but Alfred was forced to run, and he found shelter in the small marshland village of Athelney. He had the choice of being expelled from his kingdom and seeking shelter in Rome, like his brother-in-law Burgred of Mercia did, or to die at a pagan's hand, thus becoming a martyr like Edmund of East Anglia. However, Alfred chose to stay and fight, and he organized a counterattack from his hiding place in the marshes of Somerset.

The roles were now reversed, as Guthrum now sat in Chippenham like an Anglo-Saxon king, while Alfred became a raider like a Viking, waging a guerilla war against the invaders. First, Alfred reestablished communication with all of the ealdormen of Wessex that didn't surrender to Guthrum. Together, they organized a militia, which, at first, raided the Vikings in order to feed themselves, scout the situation, and remind the people that their king had not abandoned them and was willing to fight for his country. Alfred was also raiding local ealdormen who had joined Guthrum in order to show them that he still had the power to punish them. This clever game of hearts and minds Alfred played gave him the advantage, as Guthrum couldn't hope to rule the kingdom if he had no support from the local nobles, and Alfred made sure he never got that support.

The *Anglo-Saxon Chronicle* reports that Alfred met with all the leaders of his lands with all of their men at Egbert's Stone, located east of Selwood Forest. From his refuge in the marshlands, Alfred managed to raise the armies of the three shires and gather them all in the same spot, from which they launched their carefully planned attack in May 878. From Egbert's Stone, the Wessex army marched to Edington, where Guthrum had barricaded himself. The Battle of Edington went in Alfred's favor as his army proved to be victorious, but the Vikings retreated to the fortress and prepared for a siege. The Vikings were ready to apply their usual tactics of sitting it out and waiting for the negotiations to begin. However, Alfred already had experienced the Danes breaking their oaths after a treaty was achieved, and he wouldn't allow another Reading to happen. Instead, he sent his army out to pillage and destroy all the food sources the Danes could use to survive the long siege of Edington. Two weeks later, the hungry Danes sued for peace. The Vikings released the hostages and swore their usual oaths, saying that they would immediately leave the kingdom. In addition, they promised Guthrum would be baptized. That was enough for Alfred, and even though it seems that the terms were not much different than in any other treaty, Alfred had acquired the victory on the battlefield that secured the Viking's behavior.

However, it wasn't just Alfred's military organization that provided him with this victory. In the same year, the Viking leader Ubba attacked Wessex in Devon, where he was defeated by the locals at the Battle of Cynwit. Ivar the Boneless and his brother Halfdan Ragnarsson had left the shores of England, and with them, Guthrum lost their support. It was obvious that there was unrest in the leadership ranks of the Vikings, which certainly influenced their willingness to conquer the lands. In addition, Alfred did a great job of inspiring his people, and he gained the support of three shires with his efforts. Such an army, consisting of the people of the three shires, must have been much greater than the leftovers of the Great Heathen Army that Guthrum commanded.

Guthrum was baptized three weeks after the Battle of Edington, and Alfred served as his sponsor. The ceremony took place at Aller in Somerset, and Guthrum's Christian name was Ethelstan. It seems that with this conversion to Christianity, Alfred tried to impose the moral code of the Christians onto the Viking leader in hopes that, this time, Guthrum would honor his oaths. He also settled in East Anglia with the whole Viking army, at least for a while.

In 885, Asser mentions the army of East Anglia breaking their oaths and attacking Kent. But Guthrum is not mentioned by name in Asser's report. What followed the unsuccessful attack on Kent was the Treaty of Alfred and Guthrum, which firmly set the boundaries between Wessex and the Danelaw. But it appears that these boundaries were not geographical but political, as they describe where the rule of Wessex (not the land) stops and Danelaw begins. Even the term Danelaw is of much later origin, as historians needed a single name for the lands that were ruled by Viking laws in comparison to the lands that were ruled by Anglo-Saxon laws. After the treaty, the Danish lands roughly consisted of fifteen shires: Leicester, York, Nottingham, Derby, Lincoln, Cambridge, Suffolk, Norfolk, Northampton, Huntingdon, Bedford, Hertford, Middlesex, and Buckingham.

Alfred reorganized his army and started building his network of burhs, which made it extremely difficult for other Viking armies to profit from organizing raids into Wessex. By 896, the Vikings had ceased to attack; it seems as if they gave up. Some returned to East Anglia under the rule of the now baptized king Ethelstan, while others went to Northumbria. Another group returned to Scandinavia to their respective homes. Alfred's burhs proved to be so successful that they would help serve his successors in retaking the Anglo-Saxon kingdoms ruled by the Danes and uniting them under a single banner.

Chapter 9 – Edward the Elder (r. 899–924)

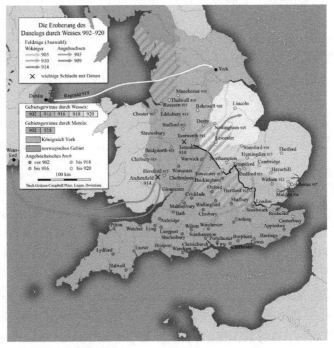

Defeat of the Danelaw in the 900s

https://upload.wikimedia.org/wikipedia/commons/4/4f/Eroberung_des_Danelags.jpg

Alfred's son, Edward, inherited the crown after Alfred's death in 899. However, even though he was the son of a king, the transition didn't go smoothly because his cousins, Ethelhelm (Æthelhelm) and Ethelwold (Æthelwold), had as much right to the throne as he did. They were the sons of Ethelred, the older brother of Alfred who ruled Wessex before him. Alfred inherited the throne when his brother died because his children were too young to rule, especially considering the kingdom faced constant Viking attacks.

Ethelhelm probably died sometime during the late 880s or early 890s because he suddenly stopped showing up in any records. He had previously witnessed Alfred's charters, and he even appeared in his will from the 880s, but his name does not pop up in the *Anglo-Saxon Chronicle* after this. His brother, Ethelwold, appeared as a witness in only one of Alfred's charters, and in it, it appears he was placed above Alfred's son Edward, meaning he was of a higher status. But Alfred was able to prepare the kingdom for his son's accession, as he promoted men who would support his son to high-ranking positions. He also continued to gift church officials, whose support was crucial for his son. Without the approval of religious leaders, it would be hard for any king to rule. In one of Alfred's charters, Edward signed as *rex Saxonum* ("king of the Saxons"). It is possible his father allowed him to rule Kent as a sub-king in order to prepare him for the succession to the throne of Wessex.

Edward was the second child of Alfred and his wife, Ealhswith. His older sister, Ethelfled (Æthelflæd), had married the ealdorman of Mercia, Ethelred. She would prove to be a good ally to her brother as she ruled Mercia after her husband's death. However, it seems Edward was closer in age to his younger sister, Ethelgifu (Æthelgifu), who became the abbess of Shaftesbury. It is unknown what happened to his younger brother, Ethelweard (Æthelweard). It is recorded that he was given the education to become a scholar, which may indicate that he was meant to join a monastery and become devoted to God. However, his children were recorded, which is proof he didn't join the church. Alfred had one more child, Elfthryth, the youngest daughter, who married Baldwin II, Count of Flanders. Asser records that the princess had the same education as her brother Edward and that she was an obedient and nice child. This marks the first time that Anglo-Saxon history records a princess having the same education as a prince.

While he was still a prince, Edward had the chance to prove himself in military leadership. He led his own troops during the renewed Viking attacks in 893 and 896, and he was successful in repelling them. At around the same time as his first command against the Vikings, Edward married Ecgwynn, his first wife, who gave birth to a son named Athelstan and a daughter whose name remains unknown, but it is known she married Sitric Cáech, the Viking king of Northumbria. Edward married a second time after his father's death to a daughter of Ealdorman Ethelhelm of Wiltshire named Elfflaed (Ælfflæd). It is unknown what happened to Ecgwynn; she might have died by the time of Edward's second marriage, or perhaps she needed to be disposed of due to various political reasons. Some historians even argue that she was Edward's lover and not his wife, but it is strange that her children would then be chosen as successors. Edward married for the third time around 919, this time to Eadgifu, the daughter of the ealdorman of Kent, Sigehelm, who had lost his life in the Battle of the Holme in 902.

When Alfred died on October 26th, 899, Ethelwold seized the royal estates of Wimborne, where his father, King Ethelred, was buried. He also took Christchurch in Dorset in his efforts to oppose Edward's succession. He declared he would rather die in Wimborne then surrender to Edward, who marched against him with an army. However, during the night, Ethelwold sneaked out of the estate and ran to Northumbria, where the Vikings accepted him as the rightful king of York. Supported by the Danes, Ethelwold attacked Mercia in 901, which was the most important ally of Wessex. On December 13th, 902, the armies, led by Edward and Ethelwold, clashed. This event is known as the Battle of the Holme, and both Ethelwold and the Danish king of East Anglia, Eohric, lost their lives during the battle. Despite losing their leaders, the Vikings won the battle, and the Anglo-Saxons suffered heavy losses. But the death of Ethelwold ended the threat to Edward's throne, and the Vikings were not interested in taking the territories.

Alfred received the formal submission of all Anglo-Saxon people that weren't ruled by Danes in 886, and his title after this recognition was *Anglorum Saxonum rex* ("King of the Anglo-Saxons"). As Edward had succeeded his father's throne, he, too, ruled all of the English people, and he used the same title in all the charters he issued except for two. In geographical terms, Edward ruled the whole Kingdom of Wessex, including Kent and the eastern provinces, but also a large part of Mercia. His sister Ethelfled, as mentioned above, was married to a Mercian ealdorman; however, it seems that Edward granted them the right to rule the land on their own. This is why some scholars prefer to think of Ethelfled as the last queen of Mercia. Edward issued charters concerning the land in Mercia, but all of them state that the rulers of this territory were Ethelred and Ethelfled. Therefore, Edward was their overlord, but he did give the couple administrative rule to some extent, as both of them issued charters in their own name.

Edward is probably one of the most neglected Anglo-Saxon kings. The main reason might lie in the fact that few contemporary sources of his rule survived. Scholars used to believe he didn't achieve much and that he didn't deserve any space in the history books. However, in the late 20th century, this opinion changed, and Edward started being regarded very highly. He might have been lesser when it came to administration or education, but his military successes were what set the scene for the United Kingdom of England. His sister Ethelfled played a huge role in conquering the southern Danelaw, and her success overshadowed Edward's in the eyes of scholars. Although Ethelfled deserves all the praise that was given to her through history, Edward was equally deserving. Edward ruled for 25 years, and he didn't just expand the realm of the English people—he also secured relative peace for the next century. The Danes were not so eager to attack once they lost their territories to Edward.

Conquest of the Danes

After the Battle of the Holme, there are no recorded conflicts between the Anglo-Saxons and the Danes. However, there is a record of Edward suing for peace in 906, and although it is not known what happened, this suggests that a conflict existed. The *Anglo-Saxon Chronicle* mentions that Edward made peace out of necessity, which implies he was in a situation where he needed to pay the East Anglian and Northumbrian Danes to leave his kingdom, just as his father Alfred did. For an unknown reason, Edward encouraged the Anglo-Saxons to buy properties and land in the territories ruled by the Danes. This might have been due to an agreement he had with the Vikings or in preparation for returning the lands to Saxon rule.

A combined West Saxon and Mercian army harassed the border between Mercia and Northumbria in 909 until they managed to acquire the bones of Saint Oswald from Bardney Abbey in Lincolnshire. This was probably the idea of Ethelfled, as she started the cult of Saint Oswald in the new minster she founded in Gloucester. Oswald was Ethelfled's predecessor and the king of Northumbria (r. 634–642). She started the cult of Saint Oswald in Mercia to satisfy the needs of the people who had relocated from Northumbria to escape the Viking rule. The Danes were forced to accept the peace with Edward, but they retaliated the very next year. They raided Mercian territories in 910 and were successful until they met the combined West Saxon and Mercian army on their way back to Northumbria. The Battle of Tettenhall followed, which the Danes lost. According to the *Anglo-Saxon Chronicle*, they lost thousands of men and two or three kings. This battle is also known as the last conflict between the Saxon army and the raiding Danes, who ravaged the English lands south of the River Humber.

After dealing with the Northumbrian Vikings, Edward was now free to concentrate his efforts on the southern Vikings, those who inhabited East Anglia and eastern Mercia. There, the Danes had founded five boroughs or main cities: Derby, Leicester, Lincoln, Nottingham, and Stamford. Each of these five boroughs was ruled by a Danish jarl (earl), but his lands around the cities were those that were used for the production of food.

Ethelred of Mercia died in 911, and his lands were ruled by his wife, Edward's sister Ethelfled. Together with his sister, Edward started building and repairing already existing fortresses around Mercia, not just to guard their lands but also to provide a base for the reconquest of eastern Mercia. After the territory was successfully taken, the fortresses served as defenses. One such fortress Edward ordered to be built was in Hertford in 912. This fortress served as the defense of London. Another one was built in Witham and yet another one in Maldon, Essex. Many people in Essex felt encouraged to bow to Edward's rule, even though they had lived in territories ruled by the Danes.

In 914, an army of Vikings from Brittany attacked the estuary of the River Severn. After ravaging the lands there, they moved toward Ergyng (Archenfield in Herefordshire), where they captured Bishop Cameleac. Edward was willing to pay a large sum for the ransom of this bishop; although it is not known why this man was so important to Edward, he paid forty pounds of silver just to free the bishop. The next year, this army of Vikings was defeated by the forces of Hereford and Gloucester. After this defeat, they released their hostages and promised they would leave these territories and never return. However, Edward was aware that the Danes often broke their oaths, and he kept an army at the Severn Estuary just in case. He was right, as the Vikings tried to attack these lands again on two separate occasions. Unable to progress, they turned their attention to Ireland. The Severn Estuary and the territories of Ergyng are in southeastern Wales, and Edward's meddling in the Viking attacks there suggests Wales was under Wessex rule by 914.

917 was the decisive year in the war against the Danes. To defend his territories from the Vikings of Northampton, Edward constructed two new fortresses, one in Towcester and the other one in an unknown place, which is recorded only as Wigingamere. During the previous year, he reinforced the fortress of Bedford when Earl Thurketil, a Danish leader, submitted to the king of Wessex. The Vikings launched an attack on all three of these fortresses but were unsuccessful in capturing them. At the same time, Ethelfled led her army to Derby, which they managed to conquer. Both events are proof that the English system of defensive fortresses was a success.

The Danes tried to imitate the Anglo-Saxons, and they constructed their own fortresses. However, there was already much disunity and lack of coordination in the ranks of the Vikings. Their fortress at Tempsford in Bedfordshire was easily stormed by the Anglo-Saxons, and the last Danish king of East Anglia, Guthrum II, lost his life there in 918. The Wessex army proceeded to take Colchester, but they never even tried to hold it. They probably didn't need this town, though, as the existing fortresses proved to be defense enough. The Danes tried to retaliate for their dead king, but Edward easily won the victory at Maldon Fort. He then returned to Tempsford to reinforce the Danish fortress with a stone wall, after which the Northampton Vikings agreed to submit to him. Soon, the armies of Cambridge and East Anglia followed, and until the end of 918, the Danish forces that resisted were in four out of five boroughs: Leicester, Stamford, Nottingham, and Lincoln.

The first to fall was Leicester, which submitted to Edward's sister Ethelfled in 918 without any resistance. The Danes of Northumbria, who had been peaceful since 910, needed Mercian protection from the raiding Norwegians who came from Ireland. They were willing to swear allegiance to Ethelfled in return for protection, but she died on June 12th, 918, and she never accepted the proposal. The Northumbrians never offered the same allegiance to her brother

Edward, and so, Northumbrian York fell under the rule of the Norwegians in 919.

The *Anglo-Saxon Chronicle* records that after the death of Ethelfled, the Mercians submitted to King Edward. However, the Mercian version of the *Chronicle* has a different story to tell. After Ethelfled's death, her daughter, Elfwynn (Ælfwynn), took her title and became the Lady of the Mercians in December 918. But soon, her uncle deprived her of all authority, and she was taken to Wessex. Nothing else is known about Elfwynn as history never mentions her again. Edward suppressed the Mercian tendency for independence and submitted it to his rule completely.

Stamford also submitted without a fight to Edward before Ethelfled's death, and afterward, Nottingham did the same. The *Chronicle* describes that all the people who inhabited Mercia, both English and Danish, submitted to Edward by the end of 918. Some of the Danish jarls were allowed to keep their lands, but others were deprived of their possessions in order for King Edward to reward his most loyal people. Some territories and estates Edward kept for himself as his private property. By 919, Edward expanded his rule to all the lands south of the River Humber, and it seems only Northumbria still resisted the unification of the whole of England. But that would soon change when Edward's son, Athelstan, took the throne after his father's death.

Edward was first recorded with the nickname "the Elder" in the 10th century in the *Life of St. Aethelwold* by Wulfstan the Cantor, who was a monk in the Old Minster of Winchester. He used this nickname to distinguish King Edward of Wessex from Edward the Martyr, who had ruled East Anglia. Edward the Elder died at the royal estate of Farndon, situated south of Chester, on July 17th, 924. The cause of death is unknown, but it could be that he died of a wound sustained during a Mercian revolt that took place later in his life. He was buried in the New Minster of Winchester, but in 1110, his remains were transferred to the new church of Hyde Abbey, just outside the city walls of Winchester.

Chapter 10 – Athelstan (r. 924–927 and 927–939)

Athelstan succeeded the throne after his father's death in 924, and as the king of the Anglo-Saxons, he ruled until 927. He became the first king of England in 927, and he ruled from 927 to 939 with that title. However, he didn't inherit the throne without some dynastic trouble. When Edward the Elder died after the uprising in Mercia, Athelstan was with him, and the Mercians accepted him as the new king. However, his half-brother Elfweard (Ælfweard) ranked higher in their father's charters, and it seems Edward might have had the intention of proclaiming Elfweard as the successor to the throne of Wessex. It is possible that Edward disposed of Elfwynn, his sister's daughter who was the Lady of the Mercians, just so he could set Athelstan as the king of her territories. Although there is no hard evidence, it seems that Edward intended to divide his kingdom and set both of his sons as rulers.

While Athelstan was accepted as the king in Mercia, Wessex probably chose his half-brother Elfweard. However, he only lived sixteen days after Edward's death. The cause of death is not known. Even though Wessex had no ruler, it seems that Athelstan still had some difficulties being proclaimed king, as his coronation was delayed until September 925. The circumstances of his succession to the throne are uncertain, but some scholars suggest Athelstan agreed to not marry or have children so that after his death, the throne would pass to his younger half-brothers. Other historians propose that Athelstan's choice to not marry came from his religious views and aspiration to a purer life. Athelstan was finally crowned in the symbolic border area between Mercia and Wessex, known as Kingston upon the Thames, on September 4th, 925.

It seems that the center of Athelstan's opposition was in Winchester, and it continued to exist there even after he was crowned. There was animosity between the king and the bishop of Winchester, Frithestan, who refused to attend the coronation ceremony. He was also never mentioned as a witness to Athelstan's charters until 928, and even then, he was listed in a low position that didn't suit his senior rank. One of the Winchester nobles, Alfred, plotted to blind Athelstan to make him inadequate to rule, but he failed. It is uncertain if Alfred acted in support of Athelstan's half-brother Edwin or if he was trying to make himself a king. It is possible that the opposition in Winchester continued to exist until 933, which was when Athelstan's half-brother Edwin died in a shipwreck. His body was taken to his cousin in Boulogne, where it was buried at the Abbey of Saint Bertin. Historians believe Edwin was running England after the unsuccessful rebellion against the rule of his brother when he died. Thus, it was probably only then that the opposition in Winchester ceased to exist.

Athelstan's grandfather, Alfred the Great, held a ceremony when Athelstan was born and honored him with a scarlet cloak, a belt decorated with gems, and a sword in a gilded scabbard. Some medieval and modern scholars believe Alfred was designating Athelstan as a potential heir, as, at the time, the king of Wessex faced a dynastic rivalry with his nephew Ethelwold. Others believe Alfred was in an argument with his own son, Edward the Elder, and that he chose his grandson Athelstan as his heir instead of Edward. There is a third theory that believes Alfred intended to divide his kingdom between his son and grandson upon his death.

Alfred was also the one responsible for sending Athelstan to the Mercian court to be educated, where his aunt and uncle, Ethelfled and Ethelred, ruled. There, Athelstan gained military training as well, which would later enable him to conquer the remaining lands of the Danelaw and impose his rule over the whole of England. It is quite possible that Athelstan remained in Mercia when his father became the king of the Anglo-Saxons as a representative of his father's interests.

When Alfred died, Athelstan's father, Edward the Elder, married Elfflaed, his second wife. It is not known if Athelstan's mother had died or if she was put aside since a new political alliance had to be made. Nevertheless, Athelstan's position was weakened due to this new marriage, as Elfflaed favored her own children as the successors to the throne. Edward had two sons with his second wife, Elfweard and Edwin, but in 920, he married for the third time, putting Elfflaed aside. His third wife, Eadgifu, also had two sons, who would later become kings. Since Athelstan never married and never had children of his own, the throne eventually passed to his half-brothers, Edmund I and Eadred, respectively.

The King of the English

The Viking king of Northumbria, Sitric Cáech, had ruled from York since 920 when he crossed the sea from Ireland to inherit the throne of his kinsman Ragnall. Even though Ragnall submitted to the Anglo-Saxon king Edward the Elder, Sitric made it quite clear that he wouldn't follow in the footsteps of his predecessor when he raided Davenport in Cheshire, which was an obvious violation of the agreement between the two nations. Nothing else is known about Sitric until Edward the Elder died in 924. However, it seems that Sitric did rule a portion of land south of the River Humber, as his coins were found in the area. These coins contradict the *Anglo-Saxon Chronicle*, which states that no Viking came south of the Humber after they submitted to Edward in 918. It is quite possible that the Vikings, under the leadership of Sitric, managed to reconquer a large area of Mercian land anywhere between 921 and 924 and that this event was unmarked by the *Chronicle*.

In 926, Athelstan met Sitric at Tamworth, where the king's sister married the Viking king of Northumbria. The two kings also made an agreement to never invade each other's territories or help each other's enemies. It was necessary for Sitric to convert to Christianity to be able to marry a Christian princess, but soon after, he reverted back to paganism. Only one year after his marriage, Sitric died of an unknown cause. He was succeeded by his cousin Guthfrith of Ivar, who was in Dublin at the time. However, before Guthfrith could arrive, Athelstan took the opportunity to invade Northumbria and seize the throne for himself. Guthfrith set sail from Dublin and tried to defend his right of inheritance, but Athelstan's army was stronger, and he easily won.

Even though Athelstan received the submission of the Danes who inhabited Northumbria, unrest followed, as they didn't want to be ruled by a southern king. The resistance to the southern rule only lasted for one year, and on July 12th, 927, King Athelstan received submission from not only Northumbria but also from King Constantine II of Alba (Scotland), King Hywel Dda of Deheubarth (South Wales), and Ealdred I of Bamburgh (former kingdom of Bernicia in northern Northumbria). There was one other king that submitted, but it remains unclear if this king was Owain of Strathclyde (southern Scotland) or Morgan ap Owain of Gwent (southeastern Wales). This event was followed by seven years of peace in the north of Britain.

Athelstan wasn't just the king of all the Anglo-Saxon people like his father. With the submission of the kingdoms of Wales and Scotland, Athelstan became the king and overlord of Britain. Many historians see his rule as the beginning of the imperial phase in England's history, which lasted between 925 and 975. Welsh sub-kings attended Athelstan's court and witnessed his charters. In fact, they were signed with a higher status than any other king or noble. It might be that Athelstan honored the Welsh rulers to justify the high taxes he imposed on their lands. For this, many Welshmen would come to resent the Saxon rule, and they even constructed a poem, "Armes Prydein Vawr" ("The Great Prophecy of Britain"), in which it is prophesied that the British would rise against their Saxon overlords and drive them into the sea.

A Problem in the North

Athelstan's position in the north was more delicate than when it came to Wales. The Scots never wanted the rule of the southern Saxon king, and Athelstan had trouble keeping his authority in their territories. The Scots always preferred to ally themselves with the pagan Vikings of Ireland, even though they accepted Christianity long ago. This means that Athelstan had to improve his position in the north in order to not lose it completely. The opportunity presented itself in 933 when his brother Edwin died and ended the Winchester opposition. The next year, Guthfrith, the king of Dublin, died, and the insecurity among the Danes started. They were in no position to send help to their allies in Scotland. For Athelstan, though, this meant the time was right to invade the north and impose his authority.

Athelstan's invasion of Scotland is briefly mentioned in the *Anglo-Saxon Chronicle* without much explanation. But the 12th-century chronicler John of Worcester claimed that King Constantine II of Scotland broke his treaty with Athelstan in 934; however, he doesn't mention the details of the treaty. Athelstan set out on a campaign in May of the same year, and with him were four Welsh kings, Hywel Dda of Deheubarth, Idwal Foel of Gwynedd, Morgan ap Owain of Gwent, and Tewdwr ap Griffri of Brycheiniog. The army was also accompanied by thirteen earls and their men, as well as eighteen bishops. Some of the earls were Danish men from East Anglia who joined their forces with the English navy instead of the ground forces.

No battles of this invasion of Scotland were recorded, and the outcome is not mentioned in any of the surviving sources. However, Simeon of Durham, in a chronicle from the 12th century, claims that the land army of Athelstan ravaged the lands as far as Dunnottar in northeastern Scotland, while the fleet raided Caithness and probably Orkney as well. Even though the outcome of the invasion is not recorded, it is clear that Athelstan managed to secure his authority over the north, as King Constantine II started signing his charters as a sub-king as early as September the same year.

However, this peace in the north only lasted for a few years. In 937, Constantine allied himself with Olaf Guthfrithson of Dublin, who had inherited the throne there and wanted to claim Northumbria as well. Backed by the Britons of the Kingdom of Strathclyde and their king, Owain, Constantine and Olaf led the attack, which was supposed to free them from the dominance of Wessex. Athelstan was surprised by their assault, as it occurred during the autumn. Typically, military campaigns in the medieval period took place during the summer. Athelstan couldn't assemble his army quickly enough, and the allies of Constantine plundered the English territories. The Welsh refused to join the West Saxon and Mercian armies, but they didn't support their British comrades either.

The main conflict between Athelstan and the alliance was the Battle of Brunanburh, which Athelstan won, preserving the unity of England. He had help from his younger half-brother Edmund, who would one day become king. Olaf was forced to return to Dublin, and Constantine returned to Scotland after losing his son in the battle. What happened to the king of Strathclyde, Owain, is not mentioned. The battle is recorded in the *Anglo-Saxon Chronicle* in the form of a praise poem called the "Battle of Brunanburh," which states that after the fighting, Athelstan and the Anglo-Saxon army pursued and slew many of their enemies. Even though Athelstan won and managed to preserve the unity of his kingdom, it seems that the resentment in the north only grew after this battle. When Athelstan died, Olaf came back from Ireland, and he managed to take Northumbria without any resistance, which shows that the people there were still reluctant to follow the southern Saxon leader.

Kingship

Athelstan ruled a wide kingdom, and he needed a modern administrative system in order to effectively govern all of its territories. As the first king of such a vast kingdom, he had to be innovative. Athelstan built a new administrative system on top of those of his predecessors, and the result was the most centralized government in the history of England. Athelstan kept the system of ealdormen, who ruled the shires and whose authority was just below the kings, in place. However, he expanded the areas that the earls controlled in order to reduce the number of ealdormen needed.

Right beneath the ealdormen were the royal officials known as reeves. This office was given to the local nobles and landowners, and they were in charge of the towns or royal estates. Medieval England wasn't a secular kingdom, and so, the Church worked together with the lay officials. The bishops and local abbots also attended the royal councils together with the nobles.

The royal council (known as the Witan) was the key mechanism of the English government. The place of the council meeting often changed, as the medieval courts did not have a permanent location. The king, his royal family, and their whole household would change locations throughout the kingdom in order to deal with arising crises. However, Athelstan mainly kept to Wessex and was reluctant to leave its borders. To deal with the problems of territories outside of Wessex, he would summon the ealdormen and nobles who were in charge there to come to him. Previous royal councils were small and intimate meetings between kings and their ealdormen. However, after the unification of England, a need for a much larger gathering of the prominent figures of the kingdom arose. Now, the royal council was attended not just by the local lords but also by the representatives of faraway territories, including bishops, thegns, and the kings who submitted to Athelstan's rule. Some historians even see these centralized royal councils as the predecessors of the Parliament of England.

In the area of law, there are many documents from Athelstan's time that have survived; in fact, more have survived from Athelstan's reign than any other 10th-century ruler. The first one seems to be the tithe edict and the "Ordinance on Charities." Scholars believe that the church officials had much to do with the writing of these laws, and it serves as evidence that the Church had an increased influence over the state during this period in history. Athelstan wrote that he was advised by the archbishop of Canterbury, Wulfhelm, and his bishops when he was writing this edict and the ordinance. The edict states the importance of paying tithes to the Church, while the ordinance regulates and enforces charity on the kingdom's reeves. The ordinance specifies the exact amount that needed to be given to the poor and also states that one slave needed to be freed annually.

As for secular laws, Athelstan considered stealing to be the greatest threat to the social order. He issued a law in which harsh penalties for thieving were introduced. Among them was even the death penalty for those who were above twelve. However, in later writings, Athelstan admitted these harsh measures didn't help much and that thieving continued to be one of the most frequent crimes in his kingdom. Desperate, he tried another strategy. Athelstan offered amnesty to the thieves who agreed to pay compensation to their victims. However, the problem of wealthy families protecting their relatives who were caught in the crime remained. One of the strategies to fight this problem was to send the criminals away from their families, often to the most distant parts of the kingdom. When the new measures didn't help either, Athelstan restored the old harsh penalties; however, he raised the age for the death penalty from twelve to fifteen, as he was concerned about how many young people were lost due to this law.

Athelstan inherited a love for learning from his grandfather Alfred the Great. Since ecclesiastical scholarship had declined during his father's reign, Athelstan was determined to reestablish its value and invest in monasteries that promoted learning. However, unlike his grandfather, Athelstan didn't care much about the general education of the people and saw the Church as the main center of education. He was extremely religious, and he often commissioned sacred manuscripts to be produced as gifts for various churches. Athelstan elevated ecclesiastical learning by bringing some of the most prominent scholars to England, among them being Israel the Grammarian, one of the most famous European scholars. He was a philosopher and a poet, but he was also the creator of a board game called "Gospel Dice," a game with a Christian spiritual concept. This game was often played at Athelstan's court, and from there, it spread around the kingdom.

Athelstan's court was where the hermeneutic style of Latin writing was revived. This style is known for its unusual use of archaic words, with the most popular words almost always derived from Greek. Many of Athelstan's charters were written in hermeneutic Latin, and the foreign scholars of his court were the most skilled practitioners of this style. Hermeneutic Latin even influenced the architecture of Athelstan's kingdom, as the builders sought to produce elaborate and enigmatic decorations for their constructions. Historians often connect this artistic style with Athelstan's ambition to show how his kingdom was successful and intellectual.

To be able to bring scholars from around Europe to work in his kingdom, Athelstan had to work hard on his relationships with the continental kingdoms. He also needed to devote special attention to the trade agreements and alliances he was making with prominent European kings. With the Carolingians, Athelstan maintained the good relations that had lasted for generations, considering his great-grandfather Ethelwulf married the Frankish princess Judith. Athelstan married one of his half-sisters, Eadgifu, to Charles the Simple, the king of the West Franks, in 919. After Charles lost his kingdom, Eadgifu sent their son Louis to her brother's court as a protégé. Later, in 936, Athelstan helped Louis regain the throne of West Francia. However, Louis, who would become known as Louis IV, wasn't the only protégé of Athelstan. Having no children of his own, he gladly took in Alan II, Duke of Brittany, as his foster son. Like Louis, Alan was expelled from his lands, and in the same year he helped Louis, Athelstan helped Alan regain his ancestral possessions.

Luckily, Athelstan had many half-sisters who he could marry to foreign rulers in order to create alliances and good relations. Hugh the Great, Duke of the Franks, married Eadhild, but not before he sent many expensive gifts to Athelstan, such as the sword of Constantine the Great, a golden crown, and a piece of the crown of thorns that Jesus Christ wore when he was crucified. In East Francia, Athelstan also created family ties that would bind him to the kingdom, as he married his sister Eadgyth to Prince Otto of East Francia, who would later become King Otto I and eventually the Holy Roman emperor.

On October 27th, 939, Athelstan died at Gloucester. Even though all of his relatives and predecessors were buried at Winchester, Athelstan didn't want it as his burial place as it was the center of his opposition. Instead, he was buried at Malmesbury Abbey, where no other member of his family was ever buried. Unfortunately, Athelstan's remains were lost in the 16th century during the Reformation, but he was commemorated by an empty tomb made in his honor.

After his death, the united English kingdom fell apart, as the Danish Vikings immediately chose Olaf Guthfrithson of Dublin as the king in York. The north still remained a problem, and the Anglo-Saxon grasp over it collapsed soon after. Athelstan's successors, his half-brothers Edmund I and Eadred, respectively, were both devoted to restoring the united kingdom. Eadred was successful in 954 when the Northumbrians removed their Viking king Eric Bloodaxe and submitted to Anglo-Saxon rule. However, Wessex was no more. Even though it remained the center of the kingdom and the main dwelling choice of its kings, it was never independent again. Unlike Mercia, which continued to show its rebellious face until the Norman conquest, Wessex was transformed completely, as if it melted away and spread itself throughout the kingdom.

Conclusion

Wessex reemerged as an independent entity after the Danish conquest of England and the rule of the Danish King Cnut in 1016. He was the one who restored the old territories of Mercia, Northumbria, and East Anglia as earldoms, keeping Wessex for himself. After only a few years, Cnut made Wessex an earldom as well, and it consisted of all the English territories south of the Thames River. Those who were chosen to be ealdormen of Wessex were some of the richest and most powerful men of England, often right after the king. The first earl of Wessex was Godwin, the father of the future king of England and the last Anglo-Saxon king Harold Godwinson. In 1066, when Harold became the king, he returned Wessex to the Crown and chose not to give it as an earldom to any of his loyal nobles. This is why 1066 is often taken as the year when Wessex ceased to exist as a political entity.

However, Wessex continued to influence the culture of England, even after the Norman conquest; in fact, it influences culture even today. Its symbol, the dragon, or more accurately the wyvern, decorated the banners of Wessex armies in 752 when it was raised in the Battle of Burford. In the modern British Army, the 43rd Infantry Division, alternatively called the Wessex Division, adopted an emblem of a golden wyvern on a black or dark blue background. In the 1970s, the Wessex region got its own flag of a golden wyvern on a red field designed by William Crampton of the British Flag Institute.

Wessex remains a term that is used to describe the historical area that consists of Hampshire, the Isle of Wight, Dorset, Wiltshire, and parts of Berkshire and Somerset. As such, it continues to inspire modern authors whose imagination touches upon old medieval times. Through captivating stories and movies, we are still able to get a glimpse of its previous glory. It can be said that Wessex was the place of the birth of Britain. However, it is remembered far beyond the British Isles, as Wessex is a part of the Scandinavian sagas, which, in their own way, describe the Viking invasion of England.

References

Ashley, M., & Lock, J. (1998). *The Mammoth Book of British Kings & Queens: The Complete Biographical Encyclopedia of the Kings and Queens of Britain.* New York: Carroll & Graf Publishers.

Ashley, M. (1961). *Great Britain to 1688, A Modern History.* Ann Arbor: University of Michigan Press.

Carruthers, B., & Ingram, J. (2013). *The Anglo-Saxon Chronicle.* Barnsley: Pen & Sword.

Finberg, H. P. (1964). *The Early Charters of Wessex.* Leicester: Univ. Press.

Keynes, S., & Lapidge, M. (2004). *Alfred the Great: Asser's Life of King Alfred and Other Contemporary Sources.* London: Penguin Books.

Young, G. M. (1934). *The Origin of the West-Saxon Kingdom.* London: Oxford University Press, H. Milford.

Here's another book by Captivating History that you might be interested in

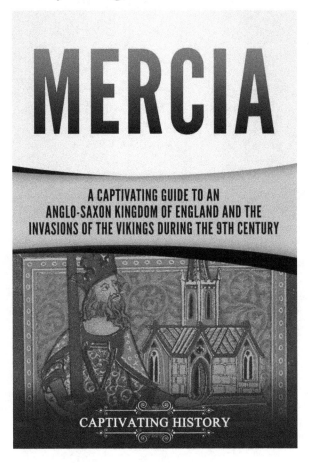

CPSIA information can be obtained
at www.ICGtesting.com
Printed in the USA
LVHW081920170620
658361LV00014B/546

9 781647 487560